A Gift for a Lifetime

And Other Stories

by

William Freeman

© 2004 William Freeman
booksonnet.com

Pelican Press
ISBN: 1888562072

A Gift for a Lifetime
And Other Stories
A book of short stories

All Rights Reserved © 2004 by William Freeman

No part of this book may be reproduced or transmitted in any form or by any means, graphic, electronic, or mechanical, including photocopying, recording, taping, or by any information storage retrieval system, without the written permission of the publisher.

Pelican Press
37 Manresa Road
St. Augustine, FL 32084
booksonnet.com

This is a work of fiction. All names and characters are either invented or used fictitiously. Any resemblance to any actual person is purely coincidental. The events described are purely imaginary.

ISBN: 1888562072

Printed in the United States of America

Dedication:

To the people I love

Cover Art

By

Starr Emerson

Table of Contents:

No Drums, No Glory	1
The Bell	22
Bad Day For The Dog	36
A Gift For A Lifetime	55
The French Broad	107
A Gift For A Lifetime II	125
Sometimes, Goat	156
Starr	160

A Gift for a Lifetime

And Other Stories

Pelican Press

No Drums, No Glory

Benny Abrams ran down Tilbury Street with his books tucked under his arm like a football. The wind was at his back. The November sky was gray and low, and bare trees lined the street. He hardly slowed at the Douglas Street intersection; a quick turn of the head spotted no cars. He leaped the curb and landed on the manhole cover in the middle of the street. He was late, but he was making good time.

His breath rushed through his lungs, and the cool fall breeze licked at the fresh scrape on his cheek. The bare trees flew by as he snatched a piece of bark from a trunk and tossed it to the wind, as he ran down the hill. His legs were strong, his wind was good and he wasn't tired. He felt that he could run forever.

Across the street, at the bottom of the hill, he could see the apartment where he lived on the second floor with his parents and grandfather. Benny wished that he could jump from the ground and fly to the window of Grandpa's room. Benny would sit on the windowsill and practice his Bar Mitzvah prayers while Grandpa lay in bed reading the Jewish newspapers.

"You're a foolish boy," Grandpa would grumble. "You're a bad actor."

"But soon I'll be a man," Benny would say.

Grandpa would smile and scratch the silver stubble on his chin. Then he would put on his skullcap and sing the prayers with Benny.

Benny stopped at the bottom of the hill to catch his breath. He hoped that Grandpa would not be mad that he was late. The afternoon had been crisp and cool. Alvin had a new football. Benny had tackled Eddie in the open field to stop a touchdown. It was a hard, magnificent tackle that had left Benny with the scrape on his face, that he now wore as a red badge of courage.

The sky grew heavier, and the wind blew across the perspiration streaking Benny's face, and it was cold. He shivered as he opened the door at the bottom of the stairway to the apartment. He expected to smell dinner in the hallway. All he sensed was dust.

Benny took the stairs two at a time, coming down hard on the ones that creaked to announce his arrival. He reached the landing and opened the door that led into the dining room.

The room was very clean. The hardwood floors were dusted and polished. The maroon print rug had been vacuumed. The table and chairs had been neatly placed together. The room seemed very bright in the light from the overhead lamp above the table.

Benny looked across the room to the darkened kitchen where he could see the wavering light of a candle, just like on the Sabbath. But this was not Friday night. His Aunt Annie came through the doorway. She was wearing an apron over her black dress. Benny walked over and gave her a kiss hello.

"Where's Mom?" Benny asked. "I'm hungry."

"Your mother is in the bedroom lying down," Aunt Annie said. "I'll fix you something."

"How's Grandpa feel?" Benny asked.

There was no sound. He looked over to the hallway where his mother was standing. She was in her bathrobe. She held a crumpled handkerchief in her hand. Her face was red, and she was crying. Benny went over and gave her a kiss, putting his arm around her shoulder. He was as tall as she was now.

"Grandpa is dead," she sobbed. "Your buddy is dead."

Benny could hardly swallow. His eyes began to water. He hugged and kissed his mother.

"I have to go hang up my jacket," Benny said and went to his bedroom.

He closed the door behind him. He lay back on his bed in the darkness with his eyes closed. He took a deep breath. He was not going to cry.

He went across the hall to the bathroom. The bright light and the white tiles hurt his eyes. He washed his face with cold water. His cheek stung. He looked at his wound in the mirror and could hardly see it. It was not important anymore.

Once, when Grandpa first came to live with them after he had gotten out of the hospital, Benny had told Grandpa that he was studying so hard for his Bar Mitzvah that he even practiced while he was on the toilet.

"Shut up," Grandpa yelled in his deep voice. "You're no buddy of mine. Bum! You do not read sacred prayers in the bathroom. Stupid! You're a bad actor."

Grandpa's look was menacing in its disapproval. He was ugly. He had a large hooked nose. Half of his face had been partially paralyzed into a frown from a stroke he had had several years ago. He was bald with a coarse gray fringe, and he wore thick glasses. Benny began to cry.

"Don't be a crybaby," Grandpa said in a softer tone. "You're supposed to be a big boy. You're going to be Bar Mitzvah. You're going to be a man."

Grandpa picked up his newspapers and walked into the living room. He sat by the window and read the Jewish newspapers. Benny watched as his large nose and thick glasses moved up and down from right to left as he read. He turned the pages backwards with his thick fingers and his large arms covered with silver gray hairs that looked like steel wool. Grandpa would cough. Without even looking away from the paper, he would take a piece of Kleenex from one pocket of his plaid robe, spit in it, and then place the used tissue into the other pocket to be deposited in the wastebasket next to his bed, later.

Grandpa was dead!

Benny stayed at home alone that night while his parents went to the funeral parlor. He would go tomorrow night. It was traditional that Jews be buried before sundown on the day of their death, but there were relatives coming in from out of town, and they would want to see Grandpa before he was buried. Benny's parents, who were not Orthodox Jews, abandoned the tradition and kept Grandpa until the family arrived so that no one's feelings would be hurt.

"My grandfather died," Benny told Alvin over the telephone.

"That's too bad. I'm sorry," Alvin said. "I guess you'll miss school tomorrow."

"Yeah," said Benny, "things aren't all bad."

"You'll miss Hebrew School and Bar Mitzvah lessons," said Alvin, "and you'll get to see all of your cousins."

"A funeral is almost as good as a wedding," Benny said.

"But not so good as a briss," Alvin said. "Hey, I got an invitation to Allen's Bar Mitzvah today. Did you get one?"

"No," said Benny.

"Did you ever get one to David's?" Alvin asked. "He's having a dinner and a band. Beverly with the big knockers is going to be there. Va va voom."

"Were not such good friends," Benny said.

"Well, you haven't lived here very long," Alvin said. "Maybe that's why nobody likes you, besides the fact you're such a schmuck."

"Up yours," said Benny.

"Anyway," said Alvin, "you're invited to my Bar Mitzvah, but you better act like a mensch, and don't puke when you get drunk."

"Very funny," Benny said.

"Is it cold out?" Alvin asked.

"Yes," said Benny.

"Then keep it in," Alvin said and hung up.

Benny sat in the living room with his cousins Winnie, Irvin, Bobby and Joan Bette. The men sat in the dining room and said Kaddish for Grandpa and then ate pastry, drank coffee, and all had a shot of whiskey. The women spent most of the time in the kitchen having a good cry and preparing food.

Benny and his cousins talked about school for a while. Then they remembered holiday get-togethers. They groaned with delight at the thought of Uncle Sam coming over for Chanukah and making candy. They took turns trying to imitate the way different relatives walked and talked. They all fell down laughing trying to imitate the way Uncle Roy snored. Uncle Harry had to come in and ask them to be quiet.

The relatives left and Benny went to bed. He looked out the window at the streetlight on the corner. Grandpa used to get off the bus on that corner when he came home from his treatments at the hospital on Friday afternoons.

"Who wants to walk to the corner with me?" Grandpa would say to Benny's mother and whichever aunt was over at the apartment at the time. There was always either Aunt Annie or Aunt Betty talking with his mother in the kitchen. They always shook their heads no to Grandpa.

"Bad actor," Grandpa would say to Benny, "you want to go?"

"Go, go," Benny's mother would say. "You stay home too much. You need to make friends. Go with your only buddy."

Grandpa and Benny would walk to the corner where the bakery was located across from the pharmacy. Grandpa would buy bread for the Sabbath at the bakery and then go across the street to the drug store to get his prescription filled. Then they would walk up the avenue to the liquor store where Grandpa would buy a bottle of brandy. Along the way, Grandpa would say hello to his friends in the stores and they would stop and talk.

"Your Catholic president is having trouble with the steel bosses," the baker would tell Grandpa.

"Kennedy is a good man," Grandpa would say. "He's good for Israel."

"So," the druggist would say, "he's a Democrat, so I voted for him. I always vote for the Democrats ever since I came to this country thirty years ago."

"He will be a great president," Grandpa would assure him. "Don't worry."

"You should be that rich president's press secretary," the liquor store man would say. "Hey, Benny, do you think your grandfather should go to Washington? So, Grandpa, what else is new? How's your health? If you haven't got your health, you are poor no matter how much money you have."

"I can't complain, knock wood," Grandpa would say and tap three times on the counter.

On the way back home, Grandpa started to cough and they had to stop.

Grandpa went to the synagogue every Friday night and Saturday morning. When he came home after services, he would eat and go to bed. At first, the whole family would go to the movies on Saturday night. Then Grandpa got sick. He was in the hospital for a while, but when he came home, he had to go back to the hospital for treatment every week.

Once he started his treatments, he didn't go out much, only to the synagogue when he felt well enough. They would all stay at home and play 500 rummy or checkers. He was one good checker player. He was the best. He beat Alvin every time they played and Alvin was on the chess team at school. Once in a while Benny could beat Grandpa, but only when Grandpa was tired. He took his medicine and went to bed.

The day after Grandpa died, Benny stayed in bed until very late. He pretended he was asleep when his mother looked in, before she went to the funeral parlor. He made his own breakfast. Then he just sat around. He didn't turn on the television, because according to Jewish custom, it was a period of sadness, and entertainment of any kid was forbidden.

Benny walked down the hall to the room where Grandpa used to sleep. The bed was made with a blue spread. The wastebasket that used to be filled with dirty Kleenex was empty. The room seemed much smaller without Grandpa.

The checkerboard was still on the night table where Grandpa kept his pocket watch. The watch was gone. So was Grandpa. Benny left the room and closed the door.

Benny had stood at the door to the bedroom and watched Grandpa carefully take off his shirt. His back and chest had red squares on them like a checkerboard. They looked like burns.

"It's from the radiation treatment I take at the hospital," Grandpa said. He pushed a jar of brown foul smelling salve at Benny. "Here," Grandpa said, "please, be a good boy. Rub it on my back. Don't be afraid. It won't bite you."

Benny took the salve. It was thick and sticky. It had an odor that smelled the way the burns looked. Benny carefully rubbed it on Grandpa's back.

"Maybe you're not such a bad actor after all," Grandpa said.

The telephone rang.

"Do you believe it?" Alvin asked.

"What?" asked Benny.

"They've killed Kennedy," Alvin shouted. "We got out early. No school 'til further notice. You're not the only one who gets to miss. I gotta go watch it on teevee. Talk to you later, dumbo."

Benny didn't turn on the television. He sat by the window trying to think. He wasn't sad. He was feeling strange. He thought he might be getting sick.

Benny's parents came home from the funeral parlor with a bunch of relatives. The television went on immediately. Dinner was made in silence, as everyone kept an ear to the teevee for the latest bulletin or rumor. It was the only thing on.

Benny went to his room. He read silently through his Bar Mitzvah prayers and his speech.

"Dear Rabbi, Cantor, honored parents and member of the congregation…"

"Not bad," Grandpa said. "Read it again. Practice. Read it again to yourself."

Grandpa was in bed. He was reading a thick blue book. It was printed in Yiddish. Benny's mother had picked it up at the library.

"What are you reading?" Benny asked.

"It's about a whale. In English, it is *Moby Dick*. Have you heard of it?" Grandpa said.

"Yes," said Benny, "we have to read it next year. Is it good?"

"Not bad," said Grandpa, "but it isn't Shalom Alechem. Now there is a good writer."

Grandpa picked up a red book from the bed. It was also in Yiddish. Grandpa opened it and smiled.

"He was from the old country," said Grandpa. "He was a very funny man."

Grandpa's smile grew broader. He began to laugh. Then he started to cough. The springs of the metal frame bed began to creak as Grandpa's shoulders heaved up and down. He could not control it. He reached out toward the night table where there was a glass of water. Benny quickly handed it to him. Grandpa sipped and held his breath. He fell back on his pillow and motioned Benny to leave the room.

The funeral parlor was dimly lit, but for the coffin. Grandpa was laid out in his "high holidays" charcoal suit. He only wore it to the synagogue on the most religious occasions. He wore it once to a wedding in New York. He also wore it to funerals.

"He looks just like he's asleep," Aunt Sophie said.

Benny did not think that Grandpa looked asleep. Grandpa looked dead. The color was painted on his cheeks. His clothes didn't have a wrinkle. Benny cautiously reached in and touched Grandpa's hand. It was cold and lifeless.

"Benny, I hardly recognized you," Aunt Sophie said. She was a big woman with huge flabby arms. She always smothered Benny's face in her bosom where Benny thought it smelled damp and moldy.

Benny and his cousins tried to imitate Aunt Sophie in front of the funeral home. They started laughing. Uncle Louie came out and told them to stop.

"What's the matter with you kids?" Uncle Louie whispered intensely. He was from the old country. He was very orthodox and spoke five languages. "Don't you have any sense?" Uncle Louie said. "And you, Benny, especially you. You're almost old enough to be Bar Mitzvah'd. You should know better. The President was killed today. We have to be careful. Times could become very bad again, even in this country. Who knows what's going to happen next?"

"We're sorry," Benny said.

Benny went back inside to see Grandpa again. They had padded Grandpa's suit. Benny knew the whole funeral parlor was fake. Even Grandpa was fake. He wasn't really there. Relatives who Benny hadn't seen in years were there. They all looked very serious as they filed past the coffin. They were all fooled. They thought Grandpa was fat.

The glass had shattered when Grandpa fell going to his room from the kitchen. He was moving slowly, when suddenly, the plaid robe collapsed in the hallway. Benny carefully stepped around the broken glass. Grandpa was trying to get up. Benny held out his hand. Benny couldn't believe how weak Grandpa had become. He was very thin. Benny felt that he could lift him from the ground with one hand. Grandpa's huge head seemed embarrassed to be carried by such a frail body. Benny helped Grandpa into bed, and then cleaned up the broken glass.

Alvin came to the funeral parlor. He wore a suit and tie under his car coat. He walked over to where Benny stood by the coffin. He shook hands with Benny very formally. He had been to funerals before. He knew how to behave. He didn't fart and he didn't laugh inside, but when they got outside, he let go a noisy one and punched Benny in the shoulder.

"Here's an impression of Jesse James," Alvin said, grabbing Benny's tie and stretching it above his head. He was a big boy and much stronger than Benny.

"Cut it out," Benny said and pulled loose.

Alvin punched him again and made a clucking sound like one of the Three Stooges.

The night was cold as they walked to the corner on the way home. There were guys hanging out in front of the bakery and the drug store. They were all talking about the assassination. They only stopped when Carol Cohen walked by in her tight skirt. She was a pretty girl with short dark hair.

"She makes my pecker hard," Alvin said.

Benny and Alvin turned the corner and walked toward the apartment.

"You're a putz," Alvin said, "a real putz. You don't know anything about the shooting of the President of the United States. I can't believe you didn't watch television because of your grandfather. When did you become so religious?"

Benny punched Alvin hard in the stomach and ran.

"I'll pound you out," Alvin yelled. He chased Benny and caught him. He hit him hard in the shoulder twice. They walked to the apartment.

"I can row a boat, canoe?" Alvin giggled.

"You're not funny," said Benny. "Do you want to come up to the apartment and eat? We have good food. Lox, smoked fish, fresh fruit…"

"Fruit," Alvin said. "How about cantaloupe?"

"I think so," Benny said.

"Cantaloupe with you, baby, you're too young," Alvin laughed.

"You're not funny," said Benny.

"I have to go home," Alvin said. "Too bad about your grandfather dying when Kennedy got killed."

"What do you mean?" asked Benny.

"I don't know," Alvin said. "No big deal. I liked your grandfather."

"He was a great checker player," Benny said.

"I let him beat me," Alvin said. "No hits back." He punched Benny in the shoulder and ran around the corner.

Benny walked slowly up the stairs. He heard the steps creak under the black rubber runner that covered them. The smell of the kosher food was warm in the stairwell. Benny's cheeks and ears burned. He could hear the television and the relatives.

They were all talking about the assassination when Benny entered the bright, overheated room. He walked around to each of his aunts and gave them kisses. He stood tall as each one examined him to see how beautiful he was, and how much he had grown since the last time they had seen him. Soon he would be Bar Mitzvah'd. Mazel Tov.

Benny shook hands with each uncle, and then let them get back to politics and whether Kennedy's death would hurt the Jews.

"I hope no Jews were involved," Uncle Sammy said.

"And no Negroes either," Cousin Mo said. "Not after all they've been through lately. It would set their cause back a hundred years."

Benny was tired of being hugged and kissed. His bedroom was being used as a coatroom. He walked by the door to Grandpa's room. He remembered how Grandpa used to talk to himself. For a second, in his fatigue, he almost went in to tell Grandpa goodnight.

"My buddy," Grandpa had said. He turned his head to look at Benny from his bed.

"Do you want anything?" Benny asked.

"A little water," Grandpa said. He had great difficulty holding himself up in bed. His arms were thin. The gray hair was now white.

Benny got the water for Grandpa. He put it next to Grandpa's pocket watch on the night table. Grandpa lay looking up at the ceiling.

"Close the door when you go out," Grandpa said, not turning his head.

Benny closed the door. He could hear Grandpa talking to himself in Yiddish.

The day was cold and wet. The wind blew rain under the green canopy with the cemetery name stenciled in white letters on the flap. The Rabbi spoke of the warm memory of the man who was struck down much as our young President had been killed. Benny felt the cold mist against his face. It beaded and ran down his cheeks. He wiped away the rain with his coat sleeve so no one would think that he was crying.

"You missed it," Alvin said on the phone. "This guy came up and shot Oswald in the guts. You really missed it."

Everyone was around the television waiting for the replay. It was too quick to be real. Benny wasn't impressed. Anyway, Alvin had told him and he knew it was going to happen.

Benny had known Grandpa was going to die. He sneaked inside and quietly closed the door at the bottom of the staircase. He was playing a game of spy in his mind. He tiptoed up the stairs. He stretched his leg to avoid the two steps that creaked. At the landing, he stopped and listened. He quietly opened the door. From the far end of the apartment, he could hear his mother's voice and Grandpa's voice rise and fall. He walked quietly through the dining room. There was crying and yelling. He went into the hallway. The door to Grandpa's room was open. Benny could see his mother leaning against Grandpa and crying.

"I'm no good anymore," Grandpa said. His voice was choked.

"No," Benny's mother said. "It was an accident."

"It won't be the last time," Grandpa moaned. "I can't even get out of bed to go to the bathroom. I wet the bed just like a baby."

"I'll get a bedpan," Benny's mother cried. "It'll be all right."

Grandpa began to cry. Benny went away.

Benny watched television. He listened to the drums. It was a glorious parade. There were leaders from almost every country in the world at Kennedy's funeral. The drums rolled. The riderless horse strained to be free. The small boy saluted. It was a magnificent tribute to the President. Grandpa always said Kennedy was a great man.

The apartment was empty. Benny's father was at work. His mother had gone to Aunt Annie's. Daytime television was dull. Benny was staying home an extra day because of Grandpa, and his mother thought he was coming down with something anyway.

Benny found his skullcap and prayer book. He would practice in Grandpa's room. Benny casually walked through the hallway to the room. He stopped and opened the door. The sun was shining through the window across the blue bedspread that covered Grandpa's bed. He walked in and looked around. He put his prayer book and skullcap on the night table next to the checkerboard. He went to the closet. His heart was beating faster. Inside the closet was Grandpa's plaid robe. He touched it. He looked in the pockets. There was some Kleenex in one pocket. In the other was Grandpa's watch. He took the watch out and began to wind it.

Benny lay back on the bed in the sunshine. He held the watch to block the sun from his eyes. He was calm.

"I miss you, Grandpa," Benny said. "There's nothing to do today. I'd like to be playing checkers with you. You were the best. I know you weren't as great as Kennedy." Benny began to cry. "I know I'm going to be Bar Mitzvah'd, and I shouldn't cry like a baby," said Benny, "but I can't help it. I love you, Grandpa."

Benny put on his skullcap and opened his prayer book. He sat in the sunlight on the edge of Grandpa's bed. He took a deep breath and wiped his eyes. He began to sing the prayers for his Bar Mitzvah.

The Bell

When they heard the bell ring, they knew that someone had died.

The two middle-aged men sat in front of the beach house in white wicker chairs on a weathered wooden deck. They watched the sun rise above the haze on the horizon. Two lines of white breakers in a blue sea rolled over the sandbars and spent themselves on the gray beach.

"You're okay as long as you hear it ring," Paul Berger said.

"It's hooked up to a direct line from the funeral home?" Bart Whitney asked refilling their glasses with the last of a gallon of wine.

"As soon as someone dies, they call him," Paul said.

They watched a heavy old man struggle up the sand dunes to the porch of the cottage next door. He was red faced. He paused to catch his breath, waved to Paul, and continued into his house.

"That's Old Al Young, the mortician," Paul said.

"Old Al Young?" Bart laughed. "I sure have been looking forward to this. While I was on that tanker in the Persian Gulf, I thought about sitting on your deck, drinking wine and telling stories and making up nicknames."

The bell rang again.

"You'll die a sailor," Paul said. "Remember the hurricane when you, me and Poison Pete tried to take that shrimp boat down to Columbia?"

"We were a lot younger then," Bart said.

"And the hurricane was only a squall," Paul said.

They both laughed and finished their drinks.

The glass doors to the house opened, and a pretty dark haired woman in a yellow caftan came out carrying a tray of cups and an espresso coffee pot.

"My Christmas Carol," Paul said and rose to kiss her.

"Did you tell Baaad Bart about our neighbor?" Carol asked as she served the coffee.

"Old Al Young, the mortician," Bart laughed and lit a cigarette.

"The bell is hooked up outside," Paul said. "He only turns it on when he goes down to the dunes."

"I suggested he get an automatic answering machine," Carol said. "They're cheap now. But, no, he wants to know right away."

"He says he likes to get them fresh, because they're easier to work with," Paul said, and he and Bart laughed.

"He's really a nice man," Carol said. "He takes the kids exploring in the dunes, and he bakes great cookies."

Carol leaned forward to give Bart his coffee, and a silver crucifix fell from the collar of her caftan.

"I didn't know you married a religious fanatic," Bart said.

"Nor did I," Paul Berger said.

"I was never very devout," Carol said. "But I haven't felt well lately. You know, everyone becomes religious when the plane begins to vibrate."

"Are you going to take the kids with you when you go to town?" Paul asked her.

"No," Carol said. "You and Bart don't mind? They're no trouble."

The bell rang again. It stopped.

"Mother, that's gross," the girl's voice could be heard before she came out onto the deck. She was blonde and trim, tan as teak. She wore a black bathing suit cut high at the hip and low at the chest. "Can't you make him get rid of that outside bell? It gives me the creeps."

"Here's Rotten Rita," Paul said to Bart behind his hand. They looked at each other and laughed.

"That's not a funny name, Daddy," Rita said. "You don't call Sophia 'rotten' or mother 'rotten'."

"Rita," Carol said. "Be nice."

"Mother," Rita protested, "he's always inferring that I'm a bitch."

"Rita," Paul said. "Be quiet. I've told you, you're not old enough to cuss until you're old enough to drive."

"Just wait until next year," Carol laughed. "I'll bet she has a couple of words for you after she gets her license."

Bart hooted and smiled.

"That's right," Rita said. She raised her eyebrows and forced a smile. "Like, ff...."

"And another thing," Paul said holding down a laugh. " I imply. You infer."

"You're weird," Rita said. "Hi, Baaad Bart."

She turned and went back inside as a sleepy-eyed tot in a nightgown ran out and hugged her mommy.

"Hey, baby Booger," Paul said.

"Hey, Booger Berger," Sophia said, and then looked surprised at Bart. "Baaaaaad Bart!"

"Sweet Sophia," Bart said and drained his coffee cup. "Are you going to be our Pakistani today?"

"Oooh bip," Sophia said and got up and poured another cup of coffee for Bart.

"You two are terrible," Carol said. "She's hardly awake. I don't want you two making her into a cabin boy while I'm gone."

"Come here, Booger," Paul said.

The little girl gave her daddy a big hug, and he kissed her.

"Mama will bring you something from town," Carol said.

"Hot dog," Sophia said.

"Don't let these two old men order you around," Carol said. "Do you want to go back to bed?"

"The bell woke me up," Sophia said.

"Are you sure you don't want me to go with you?" Paul asked Carol.

"You stay here with Bart and watch the kids," she said. "But don't get too drunk. You may have to come and get me."

"Don't worry," Paul said. "If anything was wrong, they would have called you."

"I know," Carol said.

"I'll phone the doctor right now," Paul said.

"It won't do any good," Carol said. "I tried. The girl at the office said that the doctor was in surgery and she couldn't give out any information over the phone. I have to go to town anyway to pick up more wine now that Baaad Bart is here."

"And my surprise," Sophia said.

"If you go swimming," Carol told her baby, "I want you to stay on the beach. I don't want you going out to the second sandbar. Do you understand me?"

"Oh, bip," Sophia said. "I never get to do anything."

She followed her mother inside.

"It's nothing serious," Paul told Bart. "Female problems. Probably nothing to worry about."

The day was hot and clear. The breeze disappeared. The sea became calm. The waves passed over the far sandbar without breaking. Bathers walked in the water as the sand became too hot for their feet.

"I was drinking Carta Blanca beer and tequila in the back of this van one night," Bart said. "I had to pee real bad. Poison Pete was driving and he wouldn't stop. He said, "Open the back door," I did, just as a car turned onto the road behind us. "Piss on him," Poison Pete says.

"That's Poison Pete," Paul said.

"So, I did," Bart said. "That was when I saw the blue light on top of the car. It was a damn State Trooper and boy was he mad."

"Pissed off and pissed on," Paul said.

"You two are really nasty," Rita said from the doorway. "I'm going for a walk."

"You be careful," Paul said. "Stay out of the dunes and don't talk to strangers. Do you hear me? Answer me."

"You're really paranoid," Rita said. "I'm not a baby."

She ran down to the beach before Paul could say anything. He watched as she turned cartwheels at the water's edge. Then, she headed south.

Sophia came outside wearing only the bottom half of a red two-piece bathing suit.

"I think it's time to cool off," Paul said to Bart. "Come on, Booger Baby, let's go for a dip."

"Hot dog," Sophia said.

The water at the shoreline was warm. The waves that broke on the first sandbar were knee high. The water in the deepest part of the slough was up to their chins. Sophia dog paddled between the two men.

At the second sandbar, the water ran out to waist high and rushed in around their necks. Sophia bounced on her toes to stay above the swells. Occasionally, a set of waves broke across the bar. They would dive down the face of the wave as it crested and curled riding the white water into the slough.

As Paul Berger swam back to the sandbar, he saw a large wave breaking on top of Sophia who had turned to watch him. He tried to warn her by pointing out to sea. She disappeared in the turbulence. When she came up, she was holding her nose. Her eyes were wide as she struggled for control.

"Don't panic," Paul yelled as he dove toward her.

When Paul Berger reached Sophia, she was floating on her back. Bart was floating next to her, his belly prominent in the water.

"Look at the blowfish," Sophia said.

"Whose a blowfish, you little Pakistani," Bart said and swam circles around her.

"I swallowed the ocean," Sophia said to her father and smiled.

A west wind blew horseflies down to the water, and gnats bothered their eyes. They napped fitfully through the heat of the day. Thunderheads built up over the land.

"Where are the kids?" Carol asked as she came in.

Paul Berger had been asleep on the couch in the living room overlooking the deck. The light hurt his eyes. He shook his head.

"Rita went for a walk and Sophia is taking a nap in her room," he said. His eyes adjusted so that he could see her. "Well, what did the doctor say?"

"Negative," Carol said and smiled.

"My beautiful Christmas Carol," Paul said. He smiled and his eyes were squinted and wet. He hugged her. She held onto him and began to cry. It only lasted a minute.

Paul Berger read the newspaper while Carol made a salad. Bart sat on the deck sipping a beer and smoking a cigarette. It was quiet.

A squall line began to move out over the ocean to the south of them. Lightning flashed but there was no thunder. Whitecaps began to appear on the water. The wind began to moan.

"Don't you think Rita should come home now?" Carol said.

"She'll be okay," Paul said. "She knows to come in out of the rain."

"Go look for her," Carol said.

"Can't I finish the paper?" Paul said.

"If it was Sophia, you'd call out the Coast Guard," Carol said. "You're always so indifferent when it comes to Rita."

"I don't need this argument today," Paul said under his breath. "I'll go look."

He took a pair of binoculars from a shelf near the door. He went out onto the deck and began to scan the horizon to the south. The first drops began to fall. Rita came running over the dunes in front of the rain.

"Where have you been?" Paul yelled.

"Don't be so upset," Rita said. "It really isn't raining yet."

She quickly ran inside.

"Kids!" Paul said to Bart. "Women! Three of them. Sometimes, I take off from work and sail over the horizon alone. I stay out overnight and always come back in the morning."

"I like to come ashore for a while," Bart said. "But I always return to my mistress…the sea."

They both laughed.

"Paul," Carol yelled from inside, "did you say Sophia was napping?"

The storm was moving in fast. Great gusts of rain chased the men from the deck. Inside, they got two beers. They looked out at the power of the storm, wind and rain pushing out to sea.

"She isn't in her room," Carol said.

"Where could she be?" Paul asked. "The only place she likes to go is next door with Old Al Young."

"Is he home?" Carol asked.

"I don't know," Paul said.

The bell began to ring.

"For a change, I'm glad to hear that bell," Paul said and let out a long breath. "He must be home if the bell is turned on. She's with him. I'll get her. The rain will pass in a few minutes."

The bell rang.

"I hope that they weren't caught in the dunes in this storm," Carol said. "There's a lot of lightning."

The bell rang.

Paul and Bart went out into the storm. A clap of thunder rolled down and shook the house. The wind howled. With their hands, they tried to shield their eyes as they searched through the storm.

"Help," Sophia yelled and waved from the top of the dunes to the north.

Bart pointed to her as wind and rain pushed her down the sand hill. They jumped from the deck. They ran through the whipping sea oats and tall cutting grass.

By the time Paul Berger reached the spot, Bart had already turned Old Al Young over on his back and was checking his breathing. Paul looked quickly at Sophia who was kneeling and crying. He then took a position over Al Young's chest, feeling for the lower breastbone to begin cardiac compressions. Bart indicated that there was no breath or pulse.

They administered cardiopulmonary and mouth-to-mouth resuscitation for almost a half an hour. Sophia had run home to have Carol call the Rescue Squad. They came as quickly as they could, and took Old Al Young away forever.

They sat on the deck drinking beer, watching the colors fill the sky after the storm at sunset.

"My Baby Booger did okay," Paul said. "She never panicked. They started to run back to the house when the rain began. He just fell down and she couldn't get him to get up."

"That's too bad," Bart said. "I wonder if he heard his bell?"

Bad Day For The Dog

From where he sat at the bar, he could watch the waterfront. His eyes reflected the scene. His face was sun burnt and he needed a shave. His hair was blonde, bleached white and gold in places by the sun. He was tall and thin. He sat on a tall barstool. He wore white shorts and a short-sleeved shirt open in the front. He was muscular and tan and sipped a tall glass of limewater. He was not young. He was not old. He was a man.

The boy came walking across the quay from where the schooner that brought in fruit from Martinique was docked. He was tall, dark and Semitic looking; black eyes and shoulder length black hair blown wild by the wind. He wore a tee shirt and a bathing suit. He was barefoot. He carried a small fabric bag and a spear gun. As he walked toward the bar, the sun was behind him and a white light surrounded him. When he walked in the shade, the light around him was still there.

The man watched the boy as he came into the open side of the bar facing the dock. Two women came in from the street side. They were young and

European, with sleeveless shirts and long tan legs, high heeled sandals and painted toes. One was blonde, the other brown.

The brown pointed past the boy to the harbor. The blonde's mouth fell open and she put on her sunglasses. The boy turned around to look too.

To the right of the schooner, an old blue fishing boat swung at anchor. The water was flat but for a rippled area near the bow. Everyone watched for almost a minute. Then one black head popped above the surface and then another. The second was a dog.

"So, that's the dog," the boy said. He looked at the two girls and then at the man.

"Where did you hear about the dog?" the man asked.

"I was down-island in Grenada and a red-haired guy named David on the *Firefly* told me about this crazy dog who goes diving. I'm a diver. I gotta see this. So, I caught the schooner," the boy said. He addressed the man and the two girls. He smiled, and they all smiled.

"I know David," the man said. He put out his hand. "Mitch."

"Jimbo," the boy said. They shook hands.

Mitch looked at the two girls who stood behind him. The blonde was closest to him. She had short hair and a pretty face. She had four heavy gold chains around her neck. The gold gleamed on her tan chest.

"If you fell in the water with all that gold," Mitch told the girl, "you'd sink right to the bottom."

"If I fell in," she said, "I'm sure you would jump in and save me."

The boy laughed and sat down next to Mitch. The two girls walked around Mitch and sat down next to the boy, the blonde closest to him.

"I wish I could have seen the whole thing," Jimbo said.

"Just wait till tomorrow," Mitch said. "He does it every day."

A bar girl with mahogany skin and Caucasian features stood in front of them. She smiled at the boy.

"What'll you have?" Mitch said. There was money on the bar near his glass and he pushed it toward the bar girl. "My pleasure ladies." He looked past the boy to the girls. "I recommend the pina-colada."

"They are our specialty," the bar girl smiled. She was petite, a perfect doll, wavy black hair with a red flower at one side.

"Oui," the blonde said.

"Me also," said the brown.

"Beer," said the boy.

"The usual," said the man.

The black man and the black dog walked across the quay toward the bar. Both were dripping wet. The man wore only a dark pair of shorts.

"Good day for the fish?" Mitch said as they came to the bar.

"Good day for the fish, mon," the black man said.

They sipped their drinks at the bar. The boy did most of the talking. The blonde was very interested in him and leaned close to touch his arm to stop him whenever he came to a word that she did not understand. The brown played with the wet dog while the fisherman talked with some black men at a table that overlooked the street. The man listened to the boy and watched the girl who played with the dog.

Jimbo had been diving the Caribbean, living on fish and coconuts, crewing on boats and deep diving for the precious black coral.

"There are a lot better ways to make money," Mitch said.

"The quality of life is most important," the blonde said. "Not money."

"Drinking, drugs and sex," the boy said. "That's all anybody wants to do in the islands."

The blonde girl grabbed his arm and laughed.

"And sometimes sailing," Mitch said.

"What does it mean, selling?" the brown asked and looked at the man.

"Sailing," Mitch said. "Sailing on a boat, on a sailboat."

"Merci," the brown smiled at the man. "Sailing, no selling, sailing."

"She is comic," said the blonde.

"The last sailboat I crewed on," Jimbo said, "was the *Mermaid* out of St. John, Virgin Islands. We made passage down to St. Martin. Against the sea and against the wind that time of year." As he talked he took a coin from in front of Mitch. "I had a lot of time to think about money." He closed both his hands and held them in front of the blonde. She put her hand on his left hand. He opened it. No coin. He opened the other. The coin was gone.

"Magic," Mitch smiled. "The kid is magic."

Jimbo reached his hand behind the ear of the blonde and pulled out the coin. The blonde applauded. The brown came and stood between Mitch and Jimbo.

"I want to try," the brown said.

The day ended slowly. Pink and purple filled the sky and was reflected on the bay. Black silhouettes of twenty or more boats rocked in the harbor as the colors turned gray and the water sparkled in places with the lights of the night.

Jimbo performed his magic for the ladies, making the coin vanish and appear at will. The brown rested on Mitch's knee. The blonde's face was close to Jimbo's as he rubbed the coin against his forearm. The coin fell to the bar and Jimbo picked it up. Again he tried to rub it into his arm. Again it fell to the bar. One more time. He rubbed the coin into his arm. It was gone. The girls' faces were close to him. He looked from one to the other and smiled. They both applauded. Mitch started to order another round.

"It is late," the blonde said looking at the blackness out past the quay.

"We must go," the brown said.

"Will you be here tomorrow?" the blonde asked Jimbo.

"Yeah," he said. "I want to see the dog dive. I missed most of it today."

"And you?" the brown asked Mitch.

"I'm like the dog," he forced a smile. "I do my act here every day."

The girls waved and smiled as they left.

"They come and they go," Mitch said to Jimbo.

"I thought we had something going," the boy said.

"We did," Mitch said. "We were the act for the day, the entertainment for two rich women. They're off that big yacht anchored off the casino. The men gamble all day. The women look for entertainment."

"But, what about tomorrow?" Jimbo said.

"Tomorrow is another day," Mitch said. "Come on. Are you able to drive?"

"Sure," Jimbo said. He took the coin from behind his neck and handed it to Mitch.

"No, you keep it," Mitch said. "You earned it."

The car was a dirty old green jeep. It was indistinguishable from many other old dirty jeeps on the island. There were two others parked nearby as Mitch directed Jimbo through the narrow streets that made up the harbor town. In a few small blocks, around a bend and up a hill, the town was gone. The world became defined in the headlights, a narrow black strip of asphalt, some green to the sides and then in front as the road turned.

The jeep was open with no top and as they crested the hill they came up to the sky. The stars sparkled in the blackness. Below, to one side, they could look down on the lights of the town and the harbor. The road wound down to the interior of the island. At the bottom of the hill was a large salt marsh that had a bad odor.

"Where are we going?" Jimbo asked.

"To the airport," Mitch said. "Around the marsh, just this side of the casino."

There were few cars on the road. There was no traffic at the airport.

The terminal was a long white block building. It was nighttime and it was almost deserted. A circular driveway passed under a covered entrance where Jimbo stopped. There was no one waiting. There was no one working. There was no one around.

"Keep it running," Mitch said. "I'll only be a minute."

He put on a red baseball cap and a pair of sunglasses and hopped from the car. There were four glass doors at the entrance. The first one he tried was locked. The next was open.

Inside to one side were rows of blue and red plastic seats bolted to the floor opposite a ticket counter. Two black men were there. One slept across two seats. The other stared into a bucket that held a mop as he hummed an island tune. He smoked a cigarette and paid no attention to anything.

On the other side of the terminal were a row of shops, a duty free gift store, a bar and a snack stand. All were closed and dark.

There was a lighted display window to one side of the gift store. Inside were rows of expensive watches. OMEGA. ROLEX. CARTIER. MOVADO. Mitch stood in front of the window. He looked both ways. There was no one but the two black workers.

Mitch took a slow deep breath, standing with his feet evenly apart, his knees bent slightly. He held his fists at the ready in front of him. A quick breath burst from his mouth. His left fist pulled back. The right shot forward making sharp contact with the glass. There was no great noise, just the sound of falling glass. Then, an alarm bell...

Mitch grabbed two handfuls of watches and headed for the door. He saw the two blacks. One still slept. The other turned his head slowly from the bucket but did not move forward. Mitch moved quickly out the door.

"Step on it," Mitch urged Jimbo as he threw two handfuls of watches on the floor and jumped into the car.

"What the hell!" Jimbo said and shoved the car into gear. They raced around the circular driveway and were soon back on the marsh road. Mitch threw away the red baseball cap.

"Turn right here," Mitch said.

They were off on a rocky dirt road heading up a hill. Once again they were in the world of the headlights. The rest of the world was gone. The sky above was still full of stars but they only watched the road.

"Slow down," Mitch said. "Get ready to make a right hand turn. Ready. Slow. Slow. Here. Right. Hard right. Through those leaves. Don't worry. Go. Go. Stop."

The jeep crashed through a clatter of palm fronds and stopped in front of a slab of black rock. Jimbo turned out the lights. Mitch took a couple of slow deep breaths. Jimbo stared straight ahead. Mitch started to laugh quietly as he let out a sigh. Jimbo laughed at the release of tension.

"You're a good mate," Mitch said. He picked out a large silver watch and handed it to Jimbo.

"Wow," Jimbo said, "this is a good watch. This is the best dive watch made. It's worth...." and he put the watch into his dive bag.

"It's yours," Mitch said. "But don't wear it until you get to another island. Give me a hand. I want to bury these other watches. It will be safe to sell them in about six months."

"Is this really happening?" Jimbo said.

"Here," Mitch took two white tablets from a medicine bottle. He gave one to Jimbo and took one for himself. "Put it under your tongue. It will bring you down slowly."

Mitch put the watches in a black plastic bag that he got from under the front seat. Jimbo got a shovel from the back of the jeep and started digging where Mitch indicated.

"You're a magician," Mitch said. "You know how important it is not to get caught."

"Did anybody see you?" Jimbo asked.

"One island janitor saw a white man in a red baseball cap. If he's smart, he'll grab a watch for himself and his partner and say they were both in the bathroom when it happened. The police will steal the rest. When was the last time you heard of a crime being solved in the islands?"

"I'd rather dive two hundred feet for black coral," Jimbo said.

"We all take what we can so that we can live here," Mitch said. "We're all pirates."

The next day Mitch sat at the bar as he had the day before. Jimbo came in and sat next to him. He still carried his bag and a spear gun, and a big dirty plastic bag. The pretty dark skinned bar girl came and stood in front of them and smiled.

"What do you want?" she asked.

He looked at the bar and then past the quay to the harbor. He shook his head.

"Nothing," Jimbo said. "I got no money."

"What happened?" Mitch said. "I thought you were going to get some money that the skipper of the *Firefly* owed you."

"He owes me," Jimbo said. "But he's broke too. He hasn't had a charter all month. He says he'll have money as soon as he runs a load of hootch from Jamaica."

"Another pirate," Mitch said.

"I got a job if I want to be the mate," Jimbo said. "I stayed there last night."

The bar girl brought an open beer and set it in front of Jimbo.

"It is on the house," she smiled at him.

"Thank you," he said.

"I see that you're still carrying your gear," Mitch said. "I guess you didn't take the job."

"That guy makes me nervous," Jimbo said.

"Stick with me," Mitch said. "You're magic."

"I don't know," Jimbo said. He looked around. The bar girl had moved out of earshot. There was no one nearby.

"I was thinking about hitting the casino," Mitch said.

They were both still laughing when two island Police in white jackets and blue trousers came in from the street. Their black faces were stern. They walked around the bar looking at everyone closely. They stopped behind Jimbo and Mitch.

"What's in the bag, mon?" one policeman said.

"A fish," Jimbo smiled. He bent down and picked up the large plastic bag. He put one hand down deep inside. The two policemen took a step back. One held a club.

"Take him up slow, mon," the policeman with the club said.

Jimbo slowly pulled a large grouper from the bag. It was brown with black chevrons. There was a hole in the head behind the eye. It's large mouth was a frown. Jimbo held it by the gills and turned it. The belly had been slit and neatly gutted..

"Him is a good fish, mon," the other policeman said.

"Where you be getting him, mon?" the first asked.

"Off the beach near the Casino," Jimbo said.

"You're a rich man," Mitch slapped Jimbo on the back. "Give that fish to my girlfriend here. She'll take it to the restaurant. I'd say he weighs enough to drink all night."

"What's in the other bag, mon?" the policeman with the club said. "Marijuana?"

The blonde and the brown came in from the street and added to the scene crowding in with the policemen.

"Did the dog swim again?" asked the blonde.

"Where is the dog?" the brown said.

"Fuck the dog, mon," said the cop. "Open the bag."

Jimbo looked at Mitch and made a face. He looked at the policemen. He looked around for a way out.

"There is the boat," the blonde said.

The old blue wooden boat moved slowly into the harbor. The ship that had been tied at the quay yesterday was gone. The old blue boat was the focal point. The old blue boat with the black man at the helm and the black dog on the bow.

"I gotta see this," Jimbo said. "I missed the first part yesterday."

"I seen it before, lots of times," said the cop. "It be nothing special. Open your bag."

"Just wait," Jimbo said.

"There is the dog," the brown said and moved to the bar between Jimbo and Mitch.

"Is trouble?" the blonde looked at Jimbo and the cops.

"No problem," Jimbo smiled and she smiled back and crowded next to him at the bar leaving the two policemen behind.

"Fuckin' crazy fisherman and fuckin' crazy dog," the first policman said.

"It is a sight, mon," said the other.

On the boat, the black sailor moved forward on the deck until he stood next to the dog. He bent over and lifted a heavy anchor that he dropped off the bow. Then he moved back to the helm. The dog waited forward. Slowly the boat swung with the current. The anchor rope could be seen as it stretched tight. The fisherman went forward again.

"He do what is it now?" the brown said.

"He'll dive down to check the anchor," Mitch told her putting his arm around her waist. "Make sure it holds."

There were a dozen patrons in the bar. They all watched. Men working on the quay turned to look.

The fisherman dove off the bow. The black dog waited a beat and then front paws outstretched jumped in the water with a belly splash. Then he dipped his head beneath the water and was gone.

"Unbelievable," Jimbo said.

"Incredible," said the blonde.

"I and I," the first cop said, "want to see what this long haired boy got in de bag, mon."

Jimbo lifted the bag to the bar without taking his eyes from the water. He rubbed against the blonde. She leaned against his arm.

Mitch looked over his shoulder at the two cops. The brown was between him and them. He spread his hands flat on the bar and took a deep breath. He leaned forward and looked past the chest of the brown. He watched Jimbo as Jimbo watched the water.

One black head popped above the glittering surface. The head turned from side to side. It was the man.

"Where's the dog?" Jimbo said.

The men who were seated got up from their tables and stood to watch the water. The one black head ducked beneath the sea. People on the quay walked to the edge of the dock. The buzz began to grow louder as everyone began to talk.

"Where is the dog?" The brown looked at Mitch and grabbed his arm hard.

"Is it a long time?" said the blonde.

"Fuckin' dumb dog," the cop said. "Come on up, mon. Come on up, dog."

People from the bar walked down to the quay. The policemen followed. Jimbo unzipped his bag as Mitch and the two girls started to go. He pulled out the silver dive watch that Mitch had given him.

The blonde was in front of Jimbo as they walked. She wore an oversized man's shirt that barely covered her rear end. A small gold bag swung from her arm. Jimbo caught up with her and placed the watch in her hand. She gave him a puzzled look.

"Put this in your bag, please," he said.

She hesitated, but they were into the crowd on the quay and she was too interested in the action to object.

The two policemen were parting the crowd. The black fisherman was pulled up on the dock by two men. The black dog already lay on the ground. The black man dripping wet leaned over the dog and stooped down to pick him up in his arms. He stood, turned and began to walk toward the town. The crowd made way for him. They were mostly silent. Some whispered. Some groaned.

The blonde clung to Jimbo's arm and the brown leaned on Mitch's shoulder and cried. The black man came by them with the wet dead black dog in his arms.

"What happened?" Jimbo asked.

"Bad day for the dog, mon," the black fisherman said. He continued on into town. The two policemen followed. They all disappeared past the bar.

"Bad day for the dog," Jimbo said.

The blonde was still next to him. She took the silver watch from her bag.

"Do you want me to keep this?" she asked.

"Good day for the magician," Mitch said and walked to the bar with his arm around the brown.

"Good day for the magician, mon," Jimbo said and took the watch from the blonde. He enclosed it in his fist. He opened the hand and the watch was gone.

"Bad day for the dog," she said.

A Gift for a Lifetime

Rita thought that she was fairly well experienced for seventeen years old. She had broken a couple of hearts in her time and even felt the pain of unsuccessful love once or twice herself. But all of that was in the past. Soon she would be graduated from High School. She would be leaving home. She hoped that she would be ready for the future.

She was slim and blonde. Her body was firm from years of dance lessons. Her eyes were brown, her lips thin and red. She had suffered for many years because her nose was too big and her neck was too long, but with maturity she had learned to live with her deformity. And anyway, most people said that she was pretty.

She knew she could never be as beautiful as her mother. She had mixed feelings about this. She did feel a little jealous when her boyfriends talked about what a good-looking woman her mother was . . . for her age, of course.

Even her little sister seemed prettier, well at least cuter. Sophia with her apple cheeks and freckles could really be a pain. And anytime they got into a fight, their father always blamed Rita. He always yelled at her in his big deep voice.

"I'd expect that after seventeen years you'd have enough brains to be able to get along with an eleven year old."

He was right. Sort of. He was always right. At least he thought so.

Once when she had been depressed over some boy, and it was her period, she got very hostile and refused to go to her room. When her father tried to forcibly move her, she resisted. She had been taking Karate lessons with Sophia and her mother. She was in good shape and her father was getting a little paunchy. She had lain on the floor screaming her defiance. He stood over her with his legs apart. He bent down and lifted her by her hair. She went to her room sobbing.

Later she came down and apologized to everyone. Her father showed her a few tricks he had learned in the service. There were ways she could defeat someone his size if she needed to. He wasn't angry and showed her the move gently without hurting her.

"When you were standing over me," Rita said, "I could have kicked you in the you-know-where."

"I'll remember that next time," her father smiled.

No one knew it, but it was Rita's favorite time of day. It was evening. All four of them were in the living room watching the national news. Beauty, a black mutt, had been fed and lay by the front door. Her father sat in the corner of the couch and her mother lay with her feet in his lap. Sophia sat in a chair doing her homework. She looked so pretty with her hair feathered back on both sides. She was getting so big.

Rita sat to one side and watched all of them. It made her feel good to know that they were all safe. She knew she wouldn't be with them much longer. In a few months she would be leaving the nest.

"Do you know what you can get me for graduation?" Rita said when the news was over.

Her father looked at her out of the corner of his eye. Sophia kept on doing math problems. The dog yawned.

"I know," her mother said, "a car."

"No," Rita said. "A motorcycle."

"No," her father said.

"Well, you won't give me a car," Rita said.

"A car is a big responsibility," her mother said. "By not giving you a car, we're giving you something much more. We're giving you freedom."

"But, daddy, I'm going to need transportation if I go to college or get a job," Rita said. "How about a moped?"

"No," her father said.

"They're too dangerous," her mother said.

"They cost too much," Sophia looked up.

"I'm going to be a high school graduate," Rita protested. "I'm going…"

"Then there are a few things you should know," her father said. "Learn to take 'no' for an answer. Know when to shut up. And know when to quit."

"Are you kids packed?" her mother asked changing the subject.

"I'm ready," Sophia said. "Do you think it will snow?"

"Yes," her father said.

"It would really be something," Rita said. "Plan a ski trip for two months and then have an early spring."

"It'll snow," Sophia said. "I can feel it in my bones."

"I was out in the yard today in my shorts," mother said.

"What do you think you'll get me?" Rita asked.

"I don't believe you!" her mother said. "Is that all you can think about?"

"It's okay," her father said. He looked at Rita and smiled. "I just don't want to get you any crap. I want to get you something that you can have all of your life."

"Like what?" Rita said.

"I was thinking about a good Swiss Army knife," he said.

Rita made a face and turned up her nose.

"I'd like one," Sophia said.

"Should I take a pair of heels?" Rita asked her mother.

"When in doubt, don't," her father said.

Rita stayed in the living room after they had all gone to bed. She could hear her parents laughing back in their room. There was also the sound of their television.

Sophia and the dog were asleep in the bedroom they shared with Rita.

Rita sat alone on the couch. She answered letters to her boyfriends. There were three of them now. They each swore that they loved her. All of them couldn't wait until they saw her again. They all wrote that she was beautiful. She kept all the letters in a large brown envelope in her closet. One day she had looked through them. She was surprised at their sameness. They were so repetitious. I love you. I want you. I miss you. You're beautiful. On the other hand, she wrote bright witty letters filled with her daily adventures and weekend trips.

Her family had always moved a lot. And wherever they went, they did something special. Skiing, camping, rafting, riding, sailing...

"It's going to be hard for you to find a boyfriend with as wide a range of interests as yours," her mother had told her.

"That's true," Rita said. "I do like a lot of things. I wonder why?"

"Because we've made a point to expose you to a lot of things," her mother said.

It was true. None of her boyfriends had ever been to Europe. Not even the rich one whose father was a doctor. One had visited his cousin in California one summer. But she had been to ballet school in Boston and had ridden bareback through the mountains of New Mexico. She had climbed mountains in Colorado. She had seen a five-legged cow in Kansas. She had really been around.

"That's why we can't afford to buy you a car," her mother had said.

Rita packed for the ski trip, folding her clothes into a soft red zippered bag. There was the blue and white ski sweater that Sophia had bought her for Christmas with her own money. There were the ski pants and jacket her father bought her and the new designer jeans from her mother. She was glad that they all knew to buy her clothes. She had outgrown toys long ago. She looked at her high-heeled shoes for a second. She looked back to the bedroom of her parents that was now silent. She shoved the shoes into the bag. She might meet a guy at the lodge who would take her dancing. They would go for a long walk in the moonlight. He would be handsome and strong. And they would fall in love forever.

When school got out, the white van with the blue stripe was waiting at the main entrance. The sky was overcast and it was cooler than it had been in the morning. Rita wore jeans and her maroon ski jacket. She waved as she came across the parking lot. The side door slid open and she got in. Her father had to get out and come around to close the door. It was always hard to close. He had to slide it and slam it three times before it caught. He cursed the door. He was the only one who could close it.

Her father got back behind the wheel and pulled into traffic. Across from him, her mother sat with her feet up on the dashboard. Sophia sat in a folding chair between them. Beauty sat on the floor toward the back. There was a table with bench seats built into the back of the van. The tabletop lowered onto the edge of the seats to form a large bed where Rita stretched out. Under the bed, the luggage was stored.

There were cabinets and an icebox built into the van opposite the sliding door. Her father always packed the sleeping bags inside the cabinets. There was juice and fruit in the icebox. Between the box and the front seat he stored the dirty green ponchos that they always seemed to need. Under the ponchos was his leather bag. Inside it he kept a medicine kit, sewing kit and a small black gun that he took out and kept next to him when they camped out. The gun was always loaded.

When they entered the Interstate highway, he checked out the CB radio and headed north. It was cold in the van. The heater was broken.

There was a ten-gallon plastic jug near the bunk. They used it to bring back fresh water when they went to the mountains. It was empty. Rita moved it up next to Sophia and sat on it.

Mother was singing popular songs. She had a beautiful voice. Whenever they went on trips, they would sing. Sometimes they would play a game where one person would hum a tune. The other would have to guess what it was and sing the words. Whenever Rita would hum a tune, her father would always answer very quickly.

"Blue Moon," he shouted.

"No," Rita said. "Be serious."

She hummed it again. Her mother sang "Hey Jude." Sophia sang "Darling Clementine."

They would take turns again until it was Rita's turn. She would think for a second and then begin. After one note he yelled.

"Blue Moon."

Everybody laughed.

Sometimes it bothered Rita that her father treated her differently than the others. Sometimes it made her feel good and individualistic.

Her father said that her behavior was schizophrenia caused by a hormonal imbalance due to pre-menstrual syndrome. Today as they drove she enjoyed being different. Her period was last week and her face was clearing up.

"What color is sperm?" Rita asked. She liked to be provocative even when she knew the answer.

"It depends on how old it is," her father said.

"You are disgusting," her mother told him and choked back a laugh.

"Water," Sophia said, "water colored."

"How would you know?" Rita said.

"Yeah, how would you know," her father laughed.

Sophia blushed and giggled, "I saw it on television."

"I told you she shouldn't be allowed to stay up and watch those dirty movies," Rita said.

"It wasn't a movie," Sophia said. "It was a news show about sex. They showed it and it had these little black tadpoles swimming in it."

"Those tadpoles are spermatozoa," Rita said

"I didn't watch that show," mother said. "I wouldn't have any idea."

Both girls giggled and laughed.

"Then where did we come from?" Rita said.

"Yeah," Sophia said. "Where did we come from?"

"I refuse to answer on the grounds that it may incriminate me," mother said.

"Did he park his car in your garage?" Sophia laughed.

"It wasn't a car, it was a truck," mother laughed.

"An eighteen wheeler," father said.

"Daddy, you should be ashamed of yourself," Rita said.

"No," her mother said. "He should be proud."

"It smells like snow," her father said opening the window. His ears were red. "It should be great skiing."

"I hope so," Rita said. "Who wants to go with me to the top of the mountain?"

No one answered.

The day darkened. The mountains rose as black shadows against the gray sky. Her father turned on the headlights. Snowflakes danced through the lights. They landed on the windshield, melted and were whisked away by the wipers.

They drank cranberry juice from a jug. They ate fig Newton's and granola bars. Mother peeled a grapefruit and they all shared it. Sophia had a candy bar hidden in her coat pocket. She secretly broke it in half and offered it to Rita. Rita took the larger piece without looking. A whispered argument began. Voices became louder.

"Stop it, both of you," mother said.

Her father shook his head.

"Three more months," he said.

Sophia and her mother both laughed and looked at Rita. Her feelings were hurt. She took a deep breath.

"You all can't wait to get rid of me, can you?" Rita said. "Three more months. Three more months. Well, I'll be glad to go. You all just can't wait."

"That's not true," her mother said.

"Oh yeah?" Rita said. "Daddy always says he can't wait 'til I move out."

"That's not true. He doesn't mean it," mother said.

"Wait a second," her father said. "Let's get this straight. I never said that I want to get rid of you. I'm going to miss you. You're a personality that is hard to ignore."

"Three more months," Rita said.

"I have said that I can't wait until you have a chance to get out on your own."

"See," Rita said.

"He's joking," her mother said.

"No, I'm not," he said. "It's time for her to continue her education, her life. It's time she learned about paying bills, insurance, taxes, and other people. It's time she learned the rules."

"You have too many rules," Rita said.

"It's my house," he said. "Do you really want to live with your mother and me much longer? With our rules and our bad habits?"

"Tell me about it," Sophia made a face.

"Yeah," Rita laughed. "I'm tired of picking up mother's dirty clothes all over the bathroom when she uses our shower. And Daddy, when you shave in there, there are little bitty hairs all over the sink."

"Gag me," Sophia said. "Rita, you always leave your bloody panties soaking in the bathtub."

"That's gross," her mother said.

"I don't put them in the bathtub," Rita said. "I always wash them out in the sink."

"I throw them in the bathtub when I use the sink to shave," her father said.

"Gag me," Sophia said.

"You're next," Rita pointed her finger at her little sister. "I started my period younger than you."

"Can't we talk about something else?" her father said.

"What about motorcycles?" Rita said.

"No," her mother said.

"But, I'm going to get a job after graduation," Rita said. "I'm going to need transportation."

"No," her father said. "No crap. I want to get you something you'll have for a long, long time."

"Diamonds are forever," Rita said.

"So are daughters," he said.

The snow was sticking to the windshield. It turned to ice as the wipers scraped over it. The road was hard to see. They were all quiet as father drove carefully on the winding mountain road. The night was dark and cold and full of snow when they arrived safely at the ski resort.

Their chalet was an octagonal frame building surrounded by a wooden deck. From the front doorstep, Rita looked up at the mountain. Light towers shown on the open slopes. The snow stopped. The wind quieted but snow machines howled in the distance. Their breaths flew into the air and vanished toward the stars that dotted the black sky.

Inside, the chalet was divided into one bedroom with twin beds pushed together, a bathroom with a tub, a kitchen, a dining room/living room with a fireplace and couch that opened into a full sized bed. It was decorated in yellow and white. Everything was neat and clean.

There were rules printed on a sheet of paper tacked to the inside of the front door. They had to be out by 1:00 p.m. or be charged for an extra day. They had to keep things clean. And there was a State Law that prohibited pets.

"What are we going to do about Beauty?" Sophia said.

"She'll sleep in the van like she always does," father said.

"That's cruel," Rita said.

Her mother looked at a thermometer that hung outside the sliding glass doors that led to the deck.

"It's freezing," she said.

Beauty stood outside the glass doors with her tongue hanging out and her breath making smoke.

"Let me see how cold it is," her father said. He slid open the glass door and went outside. Beauty ran inside and hid between Sophia and Rita. Mother went around the room turning on wall heaters.

Her father came back in closing the door behind him.

"It's not so cold out there," he said. "Beauty, how did you get in here? Can't you read?"

He closed the dog in the bathroom and drew the curtains by the glass doors. Then, they all went outside and brought in the food which they had brought for the weekend. Her father brought in a small television set, which he kept in the van but had never used before. He hooked it up to the cable at one side of the fireplace. He tuned it to a station that showed the weather report. Snow.

They went out to dinner at a small restaurant in a motel where they rented skis from a man named John.

"It's supposed to snow tomorrow afternoon," John said. He was a large man with a big smile. "Eight to fourteen inches. It's cold enough to make snow tonight but it'll just cover up the ice from the heat wave last week."

"Well, you know we're all beginners," her father said.

"I'm an advanced beginner," Rita said.

"I'm going to need another lesson," her mother said.

"I want real short skis," Sophia said.

John selected their skis and boots and adjusted the bindings.

"So, how has everything been?" her father asked him.

"Wednesday they were skiing in tee shirts," John said. "We haven't had a really good snow since you were here before Christmas."

"So you think we'll be okay tomorrow?" her father asked.

"Sure," John said. "The mountain is always dangerous if you're careless."

"Us beginners are always careful," her father said.

"What about you advanced beginners?" John smiled and winked at Rita.

Rita was in a giddy mood when they retuned to the chalet. Sophia had brought her small red cassette recorder and some rock and roll tapes. Rita did her robot dance, jerky mechanical movements in time to the beat. Then Sophia danced, shaking her rear end and waving her arms. Rita did her imitation of Beauty who hid under the table. Rita got down on all fours and sniffed her way around the room. She stopped and scratched her ear with her foot. Everyone laughed. Beauty turned over on her side and ignored the whole thing. Rita looked around sniffing the air. Her mother and father were seated on the couch. Mother was laughing. Father wore a broad smile. Rita crawled over to him. She sniffed at his ankle and then turned her rear end toward him and raised her leg as if to pee. Her mother laughed hysterically. Sophia rolled on the floor holding her sides. Her father rolled up a newspaper and swatted Rita across the butt.

"Go lay down," he barked.

He pushed her with his foot and she rolled over on her back with her hands and feet in the air. Her father got up and shook his leg and then pretended not to step in something. Rita laughed until her stomach hurt. Sophia crawled over to her on all fours and started to sniff. Beauty got up from under the table and left the room.

They played another tape. Her mother sang and danced. She had beautiful legs and did high kicks and turned on her toes. She had once taught a dance class when Rita was in grade school. The class put on a show for the PTA and Rita was the star.

Rita danced. Her movements were smooth, graceful, easy stretches and extensions. Her steps were light and rhythmic. Her trim well-toned body brought great expression to the form. She danced slow, serious turns, and then happy, lively leaps. Her movements filled the small room. She ended with a deep bow and everyone applauded furiously.

"Brava," her father yelled.

After the dancing, her mother and father went into the bedroom. Rita and Sophia opened the couch into a bed. Sophia fell asleep without undressing.

Rita sat up late looking out the window at the mountain. She could make out the white ski slope set against the blackness of the trees and sky. A small stream babbled by outside the sliding glass doors just below the deck. She looked at Sophia and smiled. She went over and touched her soft hair. She could hear her parents say goodnight to each other behind the bedroom door. She looked back outside at the mountain. She was very happy. She got undressed and crawled into bed next to Sophia. She pulled the covers up around her neck and went to sleep.

When Rita awoke in the morning, Sophia had already gone into the bedroom to crawl in with her parents. The first thing Rita did was look up at the mountain. The day was overcast, and the slopes were light gray.

There were two slopes and two chairlifts. To the right, an orange lift rose gradually on the beginner's slope. It was a wide path through the trees. It was well covered with man-made snow, but the surrounding woods were dark, the brown earth showed clearly between the tall green pines.

Rita knew she would have no trouble with the beginner's slope. She had had a lesson and knew how to handle the slight grade and small bumps. The thing that bothered her was the thought of all of those beginners falling down in front of her. She didn't think the slope was fast enough. She liked to fly straight down the face and then make a quick turn stop at the bottom. She loved the swoosh as the edge of her skis tossed up snow. She thought she was a good athlete and a good skier for someone who had only skied once before. She could go pretty fast without falling and she could stop fast.

In the center of the mountain were the intermediate and expert slopes. A yellow chairlift was strung through the trees to the top of the mountain. There were three places to get off the lift. The first stop half way up gave access to the wide curved area for intermediates. It was connected by a narrow path through the trees to the beginners slope on the right. There was no snow on the path, just a barren strip of earth.

The next station was three quarters of the way up the mountain, but it was hidden by the trees. The slope was narrower and steeper. Beyond that, the lift disappeared into a gray cloud on top of the mountain. According to the map on the brochure, there were two paths down from the top. One was a long trail that wound around the back of the mountain and came out just above the three quarter point. The other way was a narrow steep drop.

Rita wanted to go to the top of the mountain. She looked up into the cloud. She felt butterflies in her stomach. Maybe she could meet some cute guy who would go up there with her. Maybe there wasn't enough snow and the top would be closed. She watched the cloud, and snowflakes began to fall. A few light flakes fell to the ground and they didn't melt.

Mother and Sophia made breakfast, bacon, eggs and grits. Rita made the bed and father got out the ski gear. From a zippered bag, he handed out woolen caps and mittens. There were also scarves for anybody who wanted one. They all wore ski pants with bibs that covered their chests. Father's were black, Sophia red and Rita and Mother in blue. Mother and father both had down coats. Father had a blue one with a white stripe down the sleeve. He wore a maroon scarf and a tan wool cap pulled down around his ears. Mother's jacket was tan. Rita had her maroon ski jacket. Sophia wore a white wool sweater, a down vest, and covered them both with an orange windbreaker.

It had been Rita's job to do the breakfast dishes but she was in a hurry to get to the slopes. Her mother said that she could do them after lunch so that they would be clean for dinner. Father wanted them done "now" but mother prevailed.

There was a large wooden lodge at the base of the mountain just below the yellow lift station. Inside was a room full of wooden tables. At the back was a counter where they sold refreshments and lift tickets. There were large windows at the front that faced the mountain. There were a few people already coming down, weaving back and forth across the slope. Along the side of the slope, great fountains of man-made snow were being blown from giant nozzles.

"I signed up for another lesson," mother said. She pointed to the beginner's slope where a group was beginning to form around a tall, handsome instructor.

"Somebody go up the big slope with me," Rita said.

"I'm going with dad," Sophia said.

"We're going to start out on the beginners slope to get warmed up," father said.

Rita looked up at the big slope and then over to the smaller one. There were already people sprawled across the snow. People came down rushing out of control into the small line at the orange lift station. On the larger slope, there were fewer people and they skied faster and better.

"Alright," Rita said. "I'll go with you guys one time."

Mother went with the lesson group. Rita and Sophia rode the lift together. Her father sat with a stranger behind them. They moved up over the slope. They heard screams and laughter as people fell. The woods at the side of the slope were still bare. The snow machines roared beneath them. The sky was dark and gray and the wind blew across their bare faces. There was a small wooden shack at the top of the lift. A man sat inside looking out through a small square window. He was sipping something hot that steamed up around his face.

Rita and Sophia raised the safety bar on their chair. They lifted the tips of their skis. There was a short snowy incline in front of them as they leaned forward and the chair pushed them from behind. They slid down the little slope. Rita had her poles too low and the right one caught at the top of the incline causing her to turn into Sophia. They both fell. Rita laughed. Sophia let out a cry.

The man in the shack was supposed to stop the lift if there was an accident. But here came her father and the stranger. The stranger made a quick turn around them to the left. There was no room to the right. Her father came sliding toward them. His skis were in a wide wedge. He stopped on top of them. The ski lift was stopped.

"Are you okay?" her father said quickly looking over the situation.

Rita got up quickly. Her right pole was bent at a strange angle. Her father helped Sophia to one side. Her left ski was dragged by the safety strap around her ankle. She was crying.

"It's alright, So-So," Rita said to her sister as her father worked to get the ski back on.

"You kids have to be more careful," her father said. "What happened?"

"I don't know," Sophia said. "I just got scared."

"It was my fault," Rita said.

He looked at her and shook his head. He saw her bent pole. She turned away from his stern look.

"Let's take it easy this first time down," he said. "It looked like a lot of ice on the slopes. Who wants to go first? Okay. I'll go first. Follow me."

"I'll go second," Sophia said.

There was a sharp turn from the lift at the top of the slope. Below it narrowed and then widened into a basin at the bottom. Halfway down a huge nozzle shot snow onto the slope.

Father started out slowly across the mountain maintaining a wedge with his skis. Sophia followed behind him in identical fashion. When he got to the far side, he turned and stopped. Sophia did the same. He pointed across to where he would go on the next run. Rita came across last. She made her turn and passed them.

"See you at the bottom," her father waved. He and Sophia wedged their way across the face of the slope.

Rita headed straight down the hill. She loved the feeling of speed, the wind against her face, the whistling in her ears, the skis moving over the snow. There were a few people in her way. She saw a boy in front of her ski toward the snow machine and duck under the spray from the nozzle. Rita followed. The machine roared loudly as she ducked and flew past momentarily closing her eyes as the spray blew across her face. The boy had fallen in front of her. She went flying by just to the side of his wide-eyed face. The slope lessened, and she slowed as she passed the lesson group lined up to one side. Her mother was in a wide wedge moving carefully down the hill.

"You're doing real well, mom," Rita said as she went by.

Her mother turned to look and fell.

At the bottom of the hill, Rita made a sharp turn sideways and skidded to a stop near the lift. There was no line and she started up the lift again.

From the chairlift, she could see her father slowly going back and forth across the slope. And there was Sophia right behind him, his shadow. Rita laughed. She yelled down to them. They looked up and waved. Snow was flying everywhere. Rita didn't know if it was from the machine. She got off at the stop, keeping her tips and poles up. It was snowing. It was coming down fast. She smiled and headed down the mountain.

As Rita passed the ski school, the snow blew harder and heavier. It was blowing right into her face. She could hardly see. She was moving fast toward the bottom. There was an icy spot in front of her. Her mother was just past the spot moving toward her father and Sophia at the bottom. Rita went over the ice.

"Look out, mom" Rita yelled.

She just missed her. Rita tried to turn but it was too late. She crashed into a line of hay bales near the lift. She wasn't hurt but her heart was beating fast and her hands shook.

"What the hell do you think you're doing?" her father yelled.

"I couldn't see," Rita said.

"You could see well enough to yell, 'look out' to your mother," he said.

"It was icy," she said as he helped her up.

Her father took a firm grip on her arm and looked right at her.

"I know you can go fast," he said. "Any fool can go fast out of control. Going fast isn't skiing. I want to see that you can go slow."

"I can go slow," Rita said. Her feelings were hurt. She pulled her arm away from him. "Is it all right if I go on the yellow lift?"

He looked at her without blinking. "Okay, but be careful," he said.

"Come with me, Sophia," Rita said.

"I don't know if I'm ready," Sophia said.

"You're ready," her father said. "Just do the same thing you did here. Back and forth. The mountain is only steep going down. Back and forth, it's almost flat."

"Almost," Sophia laughed.

"I don't think Sophia should go." Mother had come over and was standing next to them.

"They'll be okay," father said. "She knows what to do."

"We'll be all right," Rita said. "I'll be with her. Why don't you two come too?"

"I'm not ready," mother said. "That lesson wasn't very good."

"I'm going to ski here with your mother a couple of times," father said. "Then I'll come over. Be careful. Don't go past the half way stop."

Rita and Sophia rode together on the yellow lift as the snow blew all around them. They looked down and saw skiers flying down the mountain and others tumbling out of control. They saw a handsome young man with the red cross of the ski patrol on his back move easily around the fallen, making sure that they were uninjured.

"He's cute," Rita said. She looked at Sophia who held tightly to the safety bar. "Are you scared?"

"Yes," Sophia said.

"Don't be," Rita said. "Remember what dad told you."

"I wish he was here," Sophia said.

There was no problem when they exited the incline at the halfway point. Rita watched as the chair moved beyond them, steeply up the mountain to the top. She and Sophia stopped and looked down. It looked much steeper than the beginners slope. But it was wider. There were patches of ice that looked yellow. There were two jets blowing snow. They had to go under the lift and over a rise to get to the wide-open slope that led to the bottom.

"I'll go first," Rita said.

Rita started down under the lift. The path was narrow and ruts had been worn where everyone had gone. She had started in a wedge, but the ruts forced her skis straight as she went up over the rise. She yelled as she was airborne. When she came down, she lost her balance and fell to the side sliding on her hip across a wide patch of ice. She laughed as she plowed to a stop in a mound of soft new blown snow. She heard Sophia scream and turned to see her come up over the rise, her arms spread like a bird. A look of surprise widened her eyes. Her mouth opened wider. She slid across the ice and tumbled into the snow next to Rita.

"Are you alright?" Rita said.

"Yes," Sophia said. She wiped the snow from her mouth. It was in her hair. It was all over her. "Did you see me? Did you see me jump?"

Rita started to laugh.

"It wasn't funny," Sophia said.

"I saw you," Rita said. She opened her mouth and eyes real wide and flapped her arms. She laughed. Sophia threw snow in her mouth. Rita threw some back. They both laughed. Two boys passed close to them.

"We better move," Rita said.

They both got up and started down the hill again.

Rita loved the wide-open area. She headed on a course where no one was and flew like the wind. She turned and passed a boy who had fallen. He smiled at her. He was cute. She skied through the softer snow at the side of the slope. It was like sand. It slowed her down. She went back toward the center. There was ice but she had no trouble keeping her balance all the way down the hill and made a spectacular swishing stop at the bottom in front of the two boys who had passed her at the top.

"You're pretty good," one boy said. "How long have you been skiing?"

"This is my second time," Rita said looking back up the slope.

"You're kidding," the other boy said. "You've been skiing for years."

"I have to go," Rita said. She couldn't see Sophia. She looked farther up. Then she looked to the side in the soft snow. There was Sophia in her wedge. Her orange windbreaker with her arms spread apart moved slowly down the mountain. Rita waited until she got to the bottom.

"That was great," Rita said. "You did real well."

"You didn't wait for me," Sophia said.

"You did great," Rita said.

"Are you going up again?" one of the boys yelled to Rita.

"Come on," Rita said to Sophia.

"No," Sophia said. "I'm waiting for dad."

"All right," Rita said. "I'm going up again. Maybe to the top."

"You better not," Sophia said. "I'll tell."

"Don't be a brat," Rita said. "I was just kidding."

Rita rode the lift with one of the boys, who was from Florida and a freshman in college.

"Are you going to the top?" she asked.

"We did before," he said. "There's too much ice. It's too dangerous."

When Rita got back to the chalet for lunch, her parents and Sophia were already there. They were eating ham sandwiches and potato chips. They drank hot chocolate. Rita stamped the snow off her boots and went inside.

"Where have you been?" her father asked sternly.

"Skiing," she said. "I met two boys from Florida."

"I thought you were going to look after your sister," he said.

"I did," Rita said. Her face started to feel warm and her ears burned. She took off her jacket and started to make a sandwich.

"Leaving her alone half way up a mountain isn't watching her," her mother said.

"I was okay," Sophia said.

"I'm sorry," Rita said.

"Sorry isn't good enough," her father said.

"What do you want me to say?" Rita turned to him. She raised her voice.

"Don't say anything," he said. He got up and came over close to her. "And don't yell at me. You were going too fast to stay with her weren't you?"

"No," Rita said. "I was just skiing. Just having fun. I like to go fast."

"You worry me," her father shook his head.

"Leave her alone," her mother said. "Let her eat."

"No," he said. "She has a bad habit of getting carried away with herself. After she's graduated and leaves home, I want to know that she can take care of herself with reasonable judgment, and not kill herself or somebody else just because she was having fun. Going fast."

"I don't need a lecture," Rita yelled back. "I said I was sorry. I can take care of myself."

Her face felt very hot and she turned and faced him directly. She stood with her feet apart. Her hands were waist high in front of her.

"Lower your voice," he said.

"Stop telling me what to do," she said.

"I'll tell you what to do," he said. "Clean up this place. Do the dishes before you go back out."

"No," she shouted. "I won't

He looked at her and smiled.

"You'll do what I tell you to do as long as you live in my house," he said.

"No," she yelled. "You can't make me."

She shifted into her karate stance. She knew she had been wrong to leave Sophia stranded alone on the mountain. She felt bad enough about it. But she was tired of being bossed around by him. She was making her stand. She was too big to spank and she knew it. And if he grabbed her by the hair…if he grabbed her by the hair, she was going to kick him where it hurt. She didn't want to injure him, just let him know she could take care of herself.

"Stop this," her mother yelled.

"Daddy, no!" Sophia yelled.

He had been facing her but now was sideways looking toward the couch at her mother and sister.

"Just leave me alone," Rita said. Her hands were in front of her. She was ready. She was the best one in her karate class. She would kick him if she had to do it.

"Do it," he said, suddenly taking a step past her right leg. His right arm came up under her arms and caught her around the chest. His right leg was behind her. He leaned forward and brought her backwards over his hip. She fell and her butt hit the floor lightly. He had held her from falling hard. His left hand caught the back of her head and kept it from hitting the wall. He looked down at her and smiled.

"I remember what happened last time," he said and kissed her on the forehead. He lifted her to her feet. "If you're going to kick somebody you better want to hurt them. And you better do it fast. After you finish the dishes, I'll go down the mountain with you and we'll see how slow you can go."

The dishes were done and Rita went back to the slopes. She stopped at the bottom of the yellow lift and looked up the mountain. The snowflakes were large now and stuck to her eyelashes. Halfway up she saw them.

Her father was in the lead in his blue coat with the white stripe. Sophia in her orange windbreaker was his shadow. Not far behind them was her mother. Father would ski across the slope followed by Sophia. They would get to the far side, turn and stop. Mother would follow. Only when she got to them, she would fall instead of turn. Father would help her up and then they would go across the same way and do the same thing on the other side. Finally as they got nearer, mother skied in a wedge directly to the bottom and stopped near Rita, almost, but not falling.

"You're doing real well, mom," Rita said. "But you don't always have to use a wedge. You can go faster if...."

Mother just shook her head.

"I'm glad you finally got off the beginner's slope," Rita said. "Will you come up to the three quarter spot with me?"

"No way," mother said. "I can't even make it from the half way mark."

Father came over followed by Sophia. He spread the back of his skis and snowplowed to an easy stop. Sophia did the same.

"So-So, come up to the three quarter spot with me," Rita said.

"No way, Jose," Sophia said. "I'm staying with mom."

"That's right," Mother said, and she and Sophia got into line for the lift.

"Will you go with me?" Rita asked her father.

"Sure," he said," but you better not leave me alone up there."

He held onto her arm as she stepped into her bindings. Then he waited while she fixed her hair under her wool cap. Then she waved to two boys and smiled. Then she was ready to go.

They hopped onto the lift, the chair coming up under them. Her father pulled the safety bar down. Rita made a face.

"Do you have to do that?" Rita said. "I don't like to feel penned in."

"I don't like to fall out," he said.

They moved up the mountain with the wind and snow blowing in their faces.

"Were those the two boys you went with earlier," he asked.

"Yes," she said.

"Their taste is a lot better than yours," he said. "They look like dopers."

Rita smiled and nudged him with her elbow.

"One of them is a musician," she said. "He said he's going to record an album as soon as he gets back to Florida."

"Do either one of them work?" father asked. "Does he get paid for his music?"

"No," she said. "He had a job as a garbage man, but his father made him quit because it had no future. And he's in school anyway. He's on the Dean's list."

"Do you believe that?" he asked.

"Why are you so suspicious?" she said.

"I just don't hold much with liars," father said. "The secret of success isn't lying. Any fool can do that. It's being able to tell the truth in an interesting way that doesn't hurt people."

The lift stopped near the halfway station. They sat swinging in the wind above the slope. The snowflakes were large and plentiful. It was sticking to the path between the slopes and in the woods.

"There's So-So," Rita pointed below them, "and mom too."

Sophia was skiing across the slope, her arms spread like an orange bird. Right behind her, mother followed. They got to the far side, turned and stopped. Mother didn't fall.

"They're both getting good," Rita said. She waved and yelled. They saw her and waved back.

The lift started up again. They kept the bar down and their skis up as they passed the halfway point. The lift headed up into the woods to the three quarter station. Rita was quiet.

The angle of their ascent increased as they passed through the trees. There was a ski instructor in the third chair in front of them. Rita looked back over her shoulder. There was no one behind them. There was a small wooden shack at the three quarter point. Rita saw it above them. She started to lift the safety bar. Her father held it down.

"We can't get off here," he said.

The ground was brown flecked with white. There wasn't enough snow. An attendant sat in the doorway of the shack. He shook his head and waved as they passed.

"What are we going to do?" Rita said.

"I guess we're going to go to the top." He said.

The top of the mountain rose above them clouded by the flurrying snow. Below, they passed over large boulders. The snow was sticking to the needles of the tall pines, but still the ground showed through between the trees. The lift stopped. The wind blew harder. Her father wrapped his wool scarf around his neck and pulled his wool cap lower over his ears. Rita zipped up her jacket and shivered.

"Daddy, I didn't want to go to the top," Rita said.

"Neither did I," he said.

She looked thirty feet below at the rocks. Her lips began to tremble. She looked off to the side so he wouldn't see that she was scared.

"This is the part I hate," he said pulling his collar up and finding little shelter from the wind. He shivered.

"Are you scared?" she said.

"Of what?" he said.

"It's so steep," she said.

"Only if you go straight down," he said.

To the left, they saw the slope. The instructor was slaloming down the face, quickly, smoothly back and forth. They could hear his skis rattle as he ran over icy spots. The lift started up again.

At the top of the mountain, there was no sun. A low cloud clung to the peak and snow swirled around them. There was a steep incline to an open area as they exited the chairlift. There was no attendant in the shack to their left. To the right, they could see the cleared trail that led around the back of the mountain gradually descending to the wide slope at the three quarter point. But large patches of brown earth interrupted the white path. They would not be able to ski there.

To the left, around the corner of the shack was the main slope. Her father had already gone to the edge. Rita pushed with her poles and slid next to him.

The slope seemed to drop straight down. It wasn't very wide. The wind blew new white snow across the yellowish ice patches. Snow clung to the sides of large bumps and mounds. To both sides of the slope, the mountain dropped away into the woods.

There were huge nozzles every fifty yards blowing manmade snow. It formed drifts on both sides.

"Look at that," her father pointed straight ahead.

Across the valley, they could see the far mountains. A mass of gray clouds was moving over the peaks toward them. Below it spread a thick blanket of white until the valley disappeared. They could not see the bottom of the mountain. They could not see the three quarter station. The snowflakes were large and could be felt as they impacted against their faces.

"It's all down hill from here," her father said.

"Daddy, I don't want to do this," Rita said.

"You can't stay here," he said.

"You always say 'when in doubt, don't,'" Rita said.

"There's a difference between doubt and fear," he said. "Don't be afraid. Be aware. You'll have to use some caution, moderation and judgment. Just stop and think. Don't panic. Figure out all the small simple steps. If you still doubt you can do all the small simple steps, then don't. But don't leave yourself up here on top of a mountain with a blizzard coming in, when there's no doubt you want to get to the bottom."

"I'll try," Rita said.

"Trying implies failure," he said. "Do it."

He pointed to a spot across the slope where the snow was blown into an embankment.

"I'm going to ski across there, just that little ways, stop and turn. Follow me," he said and pushed off. He skied in a deep wedge maintaining his balance across an icy patch hidden in the new snow. He turned at the top of the embankment, slid backwards and disappeared over the edge.

Rita was frozen as she watched him. She saw him go over the edge. Her mind flashed to the time her math teacher had been sitting on the edge of his desk. He fell over backwards. Everyone else in the class ran from the room. But Rita had been a lifeguard and a paramedic Explorer. She went up to the teacher and administered CPR until help came. She had helped to save his life. At the end of the year, he still gave her a failing grade. She may have deserved it, in Math!

Rita was moving fast across the slope. At the icy spot, her skis got in front of her and she fell backwards, but her legs were strong and she was able to pull herself forward over her skis as she plowed into the thick snow of the embankment falling forward and to the side. She caught herself with her right hand and hit a rock hidden in the snow jamming her wrist. She screamed.

"Are you alright?" her father said. She heard his voice from over the edge.

"Where are you?" Rita asked.

She saw his face as he rose over the snow mound. He was smiling.

"I waited too long to turn," he said.

"I thought you fell off the mountain," she said.

"It's only a short drop and there are plenty of trees to break your fall," he said. He pulled himself up. One of his skis hung by the safety strap.

"I think I hurt my wrist," Rita said. She took off her glove and showed it to him. He took off his gloves and felt it, gently moving her fingers. It only hurt when he bent her hand.

"You'll live," he said. He put his gloves back on and stood to get back into his skis. Then wedging himself in the snow, he helped her to get up. Her wrist throbbed as she gingerly put her glove back on.

"I don't know if I can make it," she said and tightened her grip on her poles.

"There's only one way to find out," he said. "Follow me."

He pushed off and skied back across the slope. At the far side, he turned and came back across and stopped just below her near one of the snow blowing nozzles that roared against the wind. He motioned to her to move.

Rita looked across the snow-clouded valley. She looked back at the top of the mountain that was so close yet so clouded that it was gone from sight. She pushed off across the slope. She was going too fast. At the far side, she had to fall to stop. She looked back across at her father who was waving and shouting but was drowned out by the wind and the snow machine. It was difficult but she rose and skied toward him. At an icy spot, she fell backwards and slid on her rear end to a spot just above him.

"Slow down and then turn," he yelled, "Don't forget your lesson."

He waited for her. Her wrist ached as she stood up. She pushed forward and headed for the far side. The roar of the wind and the snow machine numbed her senses. The swirl of the snow against her face and eyes made her dizzy. She slid sideways on the ice. The edge of her ski caught and she went down again. Her father stopped just below her. He waited for her and then started again.

He skied back and forth across the steep slope. He leaned forward over his skis at the bumps. He rode the ice in a controlled slide on his downhill ski. She heard him laugh a couple of times at a particularly tricky spot. She followed him. After each turn, it became easier as her legs recoiled with the bumps and danced through the turns. She squatted down as she passed under one of the snow jets. At the three quarter point, the slope widened. Expert skiers passed her going straight down the face. Her father continued to wedge and turn. Just above the halfway point, she passed him.

Her father smiled and waved and shouted something but she was gone ahead of his words. As the slope gradually eased, she could see the small crowds lined up at the lift. The snow still licked at her eyes. She straightened up leaning against her boots and swooshed smoothly to the bottom. She made a spectacular stop and looked back up the hill. She waited for her father.

"Do you want to do it again?" Rita asked him when he stopped next to her.

"Are you out of your mind?" he said.

They both laughed and headed for the lodge. They could see her mother and Sophia with their faces pressed against the window. Inside they drank hot chocolate. Her father said it was too cold on top of the mountain when Sophia said she wanted to go.

"I was scared," Rita said.

"You wouldn't be so scared if you knew how to ski slowly." Her father said.

"I know how to ski," Rita protested.

"You're a good skier, but you don't know what you're doing. It all comes too easy to you," he said.

"I saw her," her mother said. "She is good."

"It's all right to be good," he said," but it's better to be smart. Isn't that right, Sophia?"

"I want to go to the top of the mountain," Sophia said.

"Now that isn't very smart," he said. "Because you're not that good."

"It was really scary," Rita said. "I think I broke my wrist."

"Well, then can we go skiing tonight?" Sophia said.

"Not me," Mother said.

"I'm worn out," father said. "My old knees ache."

"I'll go with her," Rita said. "I'll take care of her. Please, daddy. We've never been night skiing before. My wrist isn't that bad. I can make a fist."

He looked at her for a long time.

"It's okay with me if it's okay with your mother." He said.

Her father had bought a steak and cooked it with potatoes and greens for dinner. Beauty sat next to the table with her tongue hanging out one side of her mouth. She didn't beg. She was a good dog. The windows fogged and they couldn't see the snow that kept falling. They talked about the afternoon skiing, the spills they had taken and the ones they had skillfully avoided. Rita's wrist was swollen, but nobody thought it was broken, and she did want to go skiing that night.

"I was real scared the first time I went up the big lift," Sophia said.

"Me too," Mother said. "It still scares me. I'm still a beginner."

"You should have been on top of the mountain," Rita said.

"I don't want you going up there again," her mother said.

"I won't," Rita frowned.

"It wasn't so bad," her father said. "The worst part was the cold."

"Weren't you just a little bit scared?" Rita said.

"I was concerned about how we were going to get down," he said.

"Well, I was scared," Rita told Sophia. "Daddy, don't you ever get scared?"

"Do you remember when Sophia was a baby and she had a very high fever and couldn't breathe?" he said. "Then I was scared. Do you remember when you ran away from home and didn't show up for a day and a half? Your mother and I sat there helpless. There was nothing we could do. We were both very scared. But up on top of that mountain, I knew there was something I could do about it. I could fall and slide and get up and fall again. I could always take off my skis and carry you or drag you down if I had to. I wasn't scared. Do you see the difference?"

"I do," Sophia said.

"So do I," Rita said. "Were you scared when you were in the service during the war?"

"Then, I was always scared," her father said. "And I never left the States."

After Rita and Sophia did the dinner dishes, they put their ski clothes on and went back to the slopes. It was beautiful the way the lights on the high towers cast shadows on the snow-covered mountain. The lights curved all the way to the top.

There weren't many people at the lift. The attendant said that the three quarter point was now open. Rita looked at Sophia and decided to just ski the halfway section. Her wrist was stiff. The snow had stopped and the wind was almost still. She felt full and warm. As the lift moved up the mountain, they looked back and could see the lighted road that led to the chalet. She could make out her mother and father walking hand in hand. Beauty ran along beside them.

They skied through the shadows of the night. Rita always kept an eye out for Sophia. She enjoyed chasing after her. They found a big bump that they used to practice jumping. They didn't fall much. The snow machines had been turned off. The only sound was the swooshing of skis and laughter.

Her mother and father were already in bed when Rita and Sophia got back to the chalet. The sofa bed was open. Sophia lay down and was asleep in her ski clothes. Rita sat in the dark and looked out the glass door. The lights were still on the slopes and she could see them disappear at the top of the mountain. It was beginning to snow again.

A foot of fresh snow fell that night. The next morning the sky was blue. They all skied the fresh white powder making new trails on every run. Rita skied back and forth across the slope with her mother. Her mother only fell once all morning.

In the afternoon, her father packed the van. The sun was bright and the snow was turning to slush by the time he came back to get them.

"One last run," he said.

Sophia was tired and decided that she had had enough. Mother also was ready to go. Rita caught the lift and rode to the halfway point. She thought about going further but decided against it. She skied down the slope effortlessly and flawlessly. She loved the easy movement. She loved the sun on her face and the wind in her hair.

It was beginning to get dark by the time they dropped off the skis and drove away. Sophia and mother lay on the bunk at the back of the van. Beauty was on the floor asleep. Rita sat up front across from her father who drove.

"We'll have to do this again next year," he said.

"I don't know if I'll be able to make it," Rita said.

"Oh yes," he smiled. "You will have graduated and moved out on your own. We'll be glad to have you if you can make it. You're a good person. You're a fast learner. You know right from wrong. You're a smart girl. You're pretty. I have every confidence that you'll be able to make out all right."

"Thank you," Rita said.

"I still haven't figured out what to get you for graduation," her father said.

They drove around a bend. Far off to the right, Rita could see the mountain silhouetted in the sunset. She looked over at her father who kept his eyes on the road and his hands on the wheel. He guided them safely along the winding road. Rita took one last look at the mountain as it disappeared behind them. She leaned over and kissed her father on the cheek.

"Thank you for everything you have done for me," Rita said. "That's my gift."

Her father's eyes opened wide for a second and he smiled. Without looking away from the road, he leaned sideways, turned slightly and kissed her.

"I love you," her father said.

The French Broad

We are resting today. It is Father's Day and Sunday and the day after we ran the rapids on the French Broad River.

My back aches. My left shin has a purple knot about the size of a walnut just above the ankle. Both knees have dried blood forming scabs over superficial lacerations. My right shoulder hurts whenever I do "this." So, I don't do this, I do "that," instead.

My wife is exhausted, but managing to do a book report for one of her college classes. Sophia, my eleven-year-old daughter, is running around the house imitating her cousin David who is one of the Three Stooges. My wife and Sophia both wear the marks left by the river rocks. Later, Sophia plans to take me to the movies to celebrate Father's Day.

Today, I am a father at home. Yesterday I was the Captain of the *El Dorado*, an eight foot, black rubber raft, with an all girl crew: my wife, Sophia, Lisa, an athletic young girl with thighs larger than mine, and Lynn, her quiet friend of no particular physical distinction.

We had set out with a party of forty-five rafters in ten boats with four guides. Our group included families, kids, newlyweds, older couples, and a theatrical group from Baton Rouge, Louisiana.

The brochure had said that the trip on the French Broad River was the most leisurely offered for rafting with mostly Class II rapids, a few IIIs and a couple of IVs for excitement.

We had planned the trip for a week, since my wife was going to be finished with classes on Thursday. Friday morning we had driven in our van for one hour from Spartanburg to Asheville in the mountains. We went to an antique show and shopped downtown in the shops. Asheville has a European flavor, surrounded by mountains and filled with crafts and artifacts. I bought a pair of Ibeji dolls (African) at a small antique store.

We had lunch and then drove another hour on winding mountain roads to Hot Springs to make arrangements for the white water river tour. The headquarters for Carolina Wilderness Adventures was a storefront next to the Café, across from the grocery, the Hardware Store and the Bargain Center. It was a short street. At one end was a bridge over the French Broad. At the other end were the forest and the mountains.

The tour cost $68, Sophia getting $10 off for being under sixteen. We were to meet the rest of the tour along the river at 9:30 the next morning. It would be an all-day trip, lunch included.

We bought a mess of collard greens and the best $5 steak at the Grocery, and headed for Rocky Flats Campground in the Pisgah National Park, a few miles out of town.

The campground had a large, green open area on the hillside around the bathhouse. The campsites were hidden in the woods off a dirt road that looped around the area. There was only one other family there when we arrived, so we found a secluded spot in the woods and set up camp.

We were on a mountainside that sloped gradually down through thick woods to what sounded like a bubbling stream in the distance. With our faithful dog Beauty, a flop-eared, longhaired black mongrel, as our guide, we set out for the stream. As we got closer, the grade became steeper and rockier. The rattle of the distant stream became a roar. Through the shadows of the trees, we saw a sunlit clearing just over a ledge.

It was a rocky fifteen-foot drop to the flowing creek below us. Upstream was a jagged waterfall about twenty yards across. The water rushed white and furious around the rocks. The constant torrent caused a loud beating sound, like a tom-tom, as it ran across a hollow in the ledge. Below the falls, the stream widened into quickly moving pools.

Beauty was the first to take the plunge. After carefully going in at the edge, she was carried into one of the deeper pools. The water moved her to a small falls below us that dropped around a bend. Just as we thought that she was going to be carried away, she regained her footing on the rocks that formed the falls, and walked the few feet to the near shore. She did this several times before we all stripped naked and joined her.

The streambed was treacherous, slippery with hidden rocks. Walking was impossible. We all crawled through the water upstream toward the larger falls. None of the pools was more than five feet deep.

The noise was overwhelming and constant, an explosion with no beginning and no end. The power of the water was fierce. The sun was bright and the stream was clear and warm. I managed to wedge myself between two rocks and let the falls beat a day's worth of driving out of my back. My wife and Sophia played in the falls and floated in the warm wide pools.

After the dip, we climbed back to the campsite and started dinner. We wrapped potatoes in aluminum foil and stuck them in the coals under the fire we had started. We set the collard greens in a pot of water on top of our grill. I drank wine and tended the fire while Sophia set the table. My wife rested in the van. Beauty stood watch. Her tongue hung out to the ground as I burned the steak on both sides. She waited while we ate. There was plenty left for her.

It was dark by the time we washed the dishes and doused the fire. We had brought three folding lounges and set them up with blankets and pillows. We went to bed looking up through the tall pines at the stars bright in the black sky.

It was well after midnight when it started to rain. We rushed into the van and huddled on the rubber seat cushions. By the time we went to sleep again, the rain had stopped. The air was cool and smelled of pine needles.

The next morning we woke stiff and cranky. We rode into town and had breakfast at the Cafe. The waitress was too young, bright and cheerful. We ate eggs, country ham, true grits and synthetic home fries. While we ate, we watched the place fill up with a tour group composed of potbellies, white legs, golf hats, and hairdos. They were taking the raft ride with Smokey Mountain Expeditions, the competition on the other side of the river. None of them looked particularly fit or athletic. We figured it must be an easy trip.

We drove down to the meeting spot on the river. We were early, the first ones there. We pulled into the far end of the parking area.

While I was tying Beauty to the van and setting out her water for the day, a giant motor home pulled in next to us. Stenciled on the side was Louisiana Theatrical Films, Inc. Inside we could see shadowy figures playing cards and moving about. Their generator continued after the engine had stopped. It was air-conditioned.

One by one they came out: The Director, short mustachioed; The Ingénue, pretty dark-haired with a dancer's body; The Mother of the Ingénue, an attractive blond woman with hair pulled back tight; The Tall Blonde wearing too much makeup for the occasion, The Leading Man, muscular and darkly handsome.

The Leading Lady saved her entrance for last. She was an athletically tan brunette with a broad smile. She bounded down the steps in her shorts, sneaks and tank top. She was raring to go. "Rafting, anyone?"

While we were checking out the cast next to us, the parking lot blocked from view by the motor-home, had filled up with the rest of our river party

We all boarded an old bus for a forty-minute ride over two mountain ridges. The gears ground and the wheels turned. The engine chugged and groaned. The owner, a young computer wiz with a Bachelor of Science from some eastern school, gave instructions for the wearing of the Coast Guard approved life jackets, to never be taken off once we hit the river. We sat up front and talked to him. This was his second year in business. This season was better than last. In the winter, when the weather forced him to close down, he liked to go out west and go river rafting. It beat the hell out of computers.

At the river bank, the head guide, a girl with a big smile and a lean muscular body, explained the basic skills we would need to ride the river.

Paddle "back right" to go right.

Paddle "back left" to go left.

Keep your paddle in the water. Keep paddling.

Never leave your boat.

Select a captain and get your boat in the water.

The two girls, Lisa and Lynn, latched on to us for some reason. I guess we looked wholesome. They wore athletic shorts with a name and number on them. Lisa said she had done this kind of thing before. I told her she could be Captain. She refused. I was in command.

We were heading for a Class II rapid as soon as we shoved off. I barked orders, Back Right. Back Right. Right. Back Left. Back Left. Left. Left Damn It. Left. We went sideways over the falls, bouncing uncontrolled from rock to rock. I had a crew that wasn't familiar with right and left.

My wife yelled at me, "Stop being so bossy. You act like everything is a matter of life and death."

Sophia took her side.

I had a mutiny not five minutes out of port.

"That's what I get for having women in the crew," I said.

"What did you say?" Lisa scowled.

The mutiny had spread. I had a crew in front, my wife, Sophia and me. There was a separate crew in the back giving their own commands, challenging my decision at every rock in the river. The river was full of rocks.

We navigated a couple of more Class II rapids with moderate success and then circled the boats at the shore to get instructions from the guide on our first Class III. She sketched it in the sand. There was a shoot to be approached from the left, a quick right through some boulders and then down through a shoot to the left. Beyond that the river ran wide and deep for a while.

As we approached the rapids, the rafts were strung out along the river. We were in line behind a boat carrying the Ingénue, her Mother, the Tall Blonde and a young man. We lost track of them as we struggled to control the boat in the rough water near the left bank. We were too close. A poplar branch caused us to duck.

We backed hard right to line up with the shoot. The current carried us around a large dry boulder. Dead ahead was a large rubber raft turned up on its side against a rock. Two women, the Tall Blonde and the Mother were waist deep in swirling white water hanging on to the up-turned raft.

"Back right," I yelled and nobody listened. They were all wide-eyed and open-mouthed. Their paddles were out of the water. I tried to paddle hard on the left to bring us through the shoot, but a cross current caught us and drove us head on into the stranded women.

The big black bow of our rubber boat bounced into the white thigh of the Tall Blonde.

"Sorry," I said.

"I'm glad you're not a rock," the Tall Blonde said.

The current had jammed us between the stricken raft and the dry boulder. A large rock protruding like a giant dragon tooth beneath us prevented us from being carried through a narrow shoot by the constant stream, which now was rushing in over the stern.

I quickly got the two girls forward, and we weren't swamped, though we had taken on quite a bit of water. A guide yelled from on top of a boulder at the shore to get on top of the huge dry rock next to us. Lisa carefully helped Sophia onto the rock. My wife followed and then the two girls.

I helped the Tall Blonde onto my boat, keeping an eye out to be sure the dragon tooth still held. We then tried to get the Mother, up to her neck in water, but her foot was wedged in some hidden rocks. I grabbed her life vest to steady her as she worked the foot free. The current that had rushed over our stern now ran beneath the boat. As soon as the Mother loosened her foot, the current forced her legs between our boat and the rocks below us. I still held her vest, keeping her face above the water. The Tall Blonde held her hand, and tried to pull up.

I could see downstream as one of the guides, Steve, was approaching rock by rock. He stopped when he came to the wide violent pool below the dragon tooth. He had no choice but to swim across and scale the rocks.

The raft slipped on the dragon tooth. I fell to the deck but held tight to the Mother's vest. Her face went beneath the water.

"Pull my shoulders up," she gasped as she surfaced.

I pulled as hard as I could, but the force exerted downward on the boat only wedged her tighter beneath the raft and the rocks.

"He's going to get behind you," the Tall Blonde said, excitedly out of breath, as we both pulled on the life vest. Pain and fear were on the Mother's face as a small wave splashed over her head. She closed her eyes and kept them closed.

Steve stepped into the stern of our boat. The current ran up over the transom. The boat shifted and I pulled. Steve had grabbed the Mother by the back of the vest at her butt, and she came up over the side. The boat jerked and we all fell backwards.

We were unjammed and being spit out over the dragon tooth. We bounced off the boulder as we fell. We plunged downward and the Tall Blonde fell on top of me, pinning me to the deck.

I looked back to see the Mother lying on her back in the water in the back of the boat. Steve was grabbing a paddle to control our descent.

"Can you breath?" Steve yelled to the Mother.

"Yes," she said weakly.

"Get up," I told the Tall Blonde.

"I can't," she said.

I lay on the deck with the body of the Tall Blonde on top of me. I didn't really mind. We bounded along and I watched the trees and sky jerk in and out of sight. Steve was at the stern, and he guided us to shore.

I watched over the two women on shore and bailed water while Steve went back upstream to help the other guides retrieve the rest of my crew from the rocks.

By climbing around a boulder, I could see my wife and Sophia were okay. The guides righted the capsized boat, and shortly, they were with us on the beach.

The rest of the boats joined us. We prepared to go after another boat that had overturned, spilling its crew into the river. The Mother was well enough to continue, though shaken.

My crew was shaky too, and I didn't push them through the next couple of Class II rapids. We bounded and were spun. We ran backwards over the falls. We managed to make it to shore for lunch.

My wife, Sophia and I ate together. Lisa and Lynn went off on a rock by themselves. The tour provided a picnic spread: cold cuts, potato salad, egg salad, chips, dips and lemonade. They even had good kosher pickles. We all ate and enjoyed it.

The Tall Blonde came up to me.

"Thank you for staying calm back there, " she smiled.

"What else could I do?" I smiled back at her.

"Thank you," she said.

"You're welcome," I said.

A man in a kayak brought us a couple of paddles that had been lost in the earlier mishaps. I asked him how he liked doing the river in a kayak.

"It's great," he said. "You don't have to count on a crew. You have more freedom to maneuver. I started out taking the tours in the rafts, but then I wanted something smaller, a canoe. Now all I need is this fiberglass deck underneath me."

He paddled off like a windmill, two arms turning around a head and torso connected to a sleek plastic shell.

The guide diagramed the rest of the journey. There would be two Class IV rapids. One was just ahead. The other was below mile long shallows. Another river would join us from the right, below the shallows, adding water and force to our river. A guide would go with each boat through the first Class IV.

When we set out again, I let Lisa and Lynn sit in the bow. I figured my wife and I could better control our course using my paddle as a tiller. Lisa thought it was not only a change in seating, but a change in command. I had promised my wife that I would not be unpleasant, so I quietly tried to keep us on course and follow Lisa's lead.

We made it through the first Class IV, a diagonal six-foot drop. My paddle hit a rock and the handle jerked up into my face and split my lip. I was quiet.

The Leading Lady, in a boat just ahead of us, managed to break her ankle when she was thrown from her boat into some white water below the falls. She had to choose between waiting for a helicopter to fly her out, or she could go on as a passenger and not have to paddle. She chose to go on.

Because of recent drought conditions, the river was lower than usual in the shallows. Everyone was getting stuck on the rocks in ankle deep water. The river was very wide and disappeared a mile ahead beneath a tree-covered mountain. The afternoon sun shown on the thousands of rocks that were in the river bed. There was no clear path.

With Lisa giving commands, we fell behind everyone. There was no one on the river bank but us and our boat and the rocks. We rocked and bounced and paddled. Rock to rock. Swirl to swirl. Only as a last resort would I leave the boat to pull us free of the rocks. I slipped and the water and my weight crashed my leg against a rock. The pain was sharp and I thought for a second that it was broken. No such luck. I kept paddling and pushing.

I saw where the river was joined by another far to the right. The mountain in front of us grew larger, towering above the river valley, a rising emerald mass, with a white granite scar a hundred yards high marking its right slope.

After endless rocks and pain, we made it to the joining river and rushed around the base of the mountain to where a guide waited for us at the second Class IV. The other boats were at the shore receiving directions for the assault. Two guides would be needed to stand in the shallow water above the falls and help push us through, so we would have to navigate alone.

Lisa wanted to wait, but I ordered us into line and we headed for the falls. The boat ahead of us was stuck so we back paddled waiting our turn. We saw the boat disappear and heard screams and then cheers as they came out the shoot below.

We paddled straight for the first guide. Our approach was perfect. The guide shoved us across to the other guide.

"Paddle hard. Hard," I yelled.

"Hard, hard," yelled Sophia.

"Paddle, paddle," my wife yelled.

We all paddled furiously to cross the rocks at the head of the falls. We went over. Down. Down a four foot straight drop and crashed against the boulder.

"Paddle, paddle," my wife yelled.

"Hard, hard," yelled Sophia.

A whirlpool spun us.

"Hard right," I yelled and could see my wife paddling with all her strength next to me.

We came about, and the river shot us over another falls to our right. We passed backwards through a shoot, and spun out into deeper, calmer waters. We all cheered. We paddled to shore.

My wife was worn out and dropped over the side for a quick cooling dip. The change in weight caused the boat to veer. My wife grabbed a line on the boat and we all spun from the shore toward the rocks further down. My wife was between the rocks and the boat that the river was about to crush on top of her.

I backed hard left and yelled to paddle hard right.

"Right, right," I yelled.

The boat came about pulling my wife out of the way as the stern crashed against the rocks. Sophia grabbed her mother's hand and I grabbed the back of her life vest and landed her in the boat.

We paddled hard and beached the boat just below the boulders. I bailed the boat while the rest of the crew went up on the rocks to cheer the rest of our party through the rapids. Even the guided boats had trouble. Ours had been one of the cleaner conquests.

The remainder of the trip was difficult but not threatening. The river was very low and we wound up on more rocks than we should have, but we overcame each obstacle without having to leave the boat. There was no danger.

When we could see the bridge at Hot Springs, we laughed and enjoyed the final scenery, dark green mountains and water sparkling in the late day sun at our backs. Sophia took over her mother's paddle for the last mile and a half. She did very well. She was the freshest of the crew. We were all sunburned and tired. We were bruised and lacerated. The river had left its mark on all of us.

As we paddled under the bridge, we saw a black swastika painted on one of the concrete abutments.

The Leading Lady was carried to the bus. She still had a smile. She waited quietly with the Leading Man.

We carried our raft on top of our heads up the embankment. One of our guides pulled the plug. There was a great whoosh of air and the *El Dorado* collapsed, limp and wrinkled on a stack of other deflated black boats.

It is Sunday, Father's Day, and Sophia has promised to take me to the movies with her own money. She wants to see Raiders of the Lost Ark. She says it is an adventure film.

A Gift for a Lifetime II

When Sophia's older sister Rita graduated from high school, Dad had written a story as her graduation gift. The story contained a moral, which Sophia thought Rita needed for growing up. Sophia needed to finish her home-study course in geometry, and then she would also have her diploma. She wondered what her father's gift to her would be.

Their boat was a forty-foot trimaran which Mom had renamed *Riphia*, combining her children's names. It was supposed to be bad luck to change the name of a boat, but Mom was not superstitious. She said that her love for Rita and Sophia was stronger than any demons the sea could create.

The whole family would be together again. Just like in the old days at home before the girls had departed the nest, there would be only the four of them on the boat.

It was late summer and hurricane season. They were going to be in the Bermuda Triangle. Sophia wasn't the least bit nervous. She knew that Dad would not have planned the cruise for the family if it was dangerous.

For the past year, while her parents had been working on the boat, Sophia had been living with her grandmother in the country, finishing high school by correspondence. She would be going to college in the fall. Rita was already a sophomore in California. It was to be a grand reunion. Sophia was thrilled with anticipation.

Sophia wore a one-piece gray bathing suit and sat on her bunk in the aft cabin of the trimaran. She was drawing. She tried to keep her sketchpad in the shade, but the boat was swinging and the sunlight through the large overhead hatch kept following her. Then it began to rain.

"This is crazy," Sophia talked aloud. "The sun is shining and it's raining. Is the whole trip going to be like this?"

She closed her hatch and then closed the hatch above the starboard berth across from the galley. By the time she got to the companionway leading to the big center cockpit, the rain had stopped. She ducked out from under the canopy that shaded the cockpit. It was hot and bright on the wide deck. Sophia stepped over the double lifelines and stainless steel stanchions that rimmed the entire boat and dove into the water.

The water was warm. There was no shock as she splashed into the bay. From air to water was a change of elements without a change of temperature. It was magic. She dove to the bottom. She opened her eyes and saw dots of raindrops on the surface. She kicked upward with her head back as she surfaced so that her hair flowed away from her face. She swam through the cool raindrops. The sun shone brightly.

Sophia saw the gray dinghy coming out the channel. Her parents had met Rita at the airport. She was sitting in the bow of the boat waving frantically. They hadn't always gotten along, but there was an eternal sisterly love that they shared forever.

Sophia held on to the rubber dinghy. Rita leaned over the side and kissed her. The small boat heeled over badly but did not capsize. Sophia saw four large suitcases resting between her mother and father. Dad was frowning as he lifted a heavy bag so that mother could get on deck to tie off the rope from the dinghy.

There was a galley and two berths in the aft cabin, which Rita and Sophia shared, along with the four suitcases. Sophia sat on the counter across from the propane stove. Rita began to unpack.

"I only brought one bag," Sophia said.

"Alright already," Rita said. "Don't make a big deal out of it. I didn't know what to wear, so I brought it all."

Dad stuck his head in through the companionway. He looked around the messy cabin and shook his head. He still frowned.

"Travel light," he said. It was a commandment. "The wind will be out of the west tonight. There will be a full moon too. Let's get the boat ready to go."

Sophia was underwater scraping the barnacles from the outer hulls when the engine stopped.

Dad took it the hardest when the engine broke down. He had really wanted to go sailing with his "all girl crew." He swore and cursed all the way to shore in the dinghy. Everyone else was quiet.

Finally Mother interrupted his tirade. "You don't have any control over what happens in your life," she said. "The only thing you can control is your attitude."

"That's right," Rita said. "Life is a movie. We are only actors. Someone else has written the script."

"All the world is a stage," Dad said. "Shakespeare wrote that."

"That's because they didn't have movies back then," Rita said.

"It was going to be a great adventure on the high seas," Dad said but he wasn't smiling.

"Then, it'll just have to be a different story," Sophia said.

"A different story," Dad said, and winked at her. "How's your geometry coming along?"

Sophia's father had begun a story about her years ago. She remembered him sitting at the typewriter, smiling, in the office he had built in the garage. But it was "lost in the shuffle" when they moved to New York. He liked to believe that it was stolen by a secret admirer. But Sophia thought it was probably thrown out in the trash with the broken boxes and crumpled newspapers used to pack the dishes.

The story was about a deep sea fishing trip that the two of them had gone on together when she was eleven. It was a large party boat with thirty other people. Sophia had served Dad beer from the ice chest, while he played poker with a rowdy group in the cabin, on the way out and back. He won enough money to buy her a tee shirt with a picture of the party boat on the back.

In between the action of the card games, Sophia had hooked a big fish, which Dad had landed. It was a large blue and silver bonita, which flashed green light from its slick wetback as it struggled on deck. It was the biggest fish of the day and there was a disagreement as to whether or not it qualified for the pool that her father had entered. There was over a hundred dollars in the pot. Then some old geezer landed a big silver pompano late in the day, so Sophia and Dad settled for second best.

They had walked home along the seawall. Sophia followed Dad's footsteps. He wore his old Army shorts and his old four-pocket blue shirt that Mom had tried to throw away. Sophia knew what he had in every pocket, where he kept his money, and where he kept the Swiss army knife that she had bought him for Father's Day when they lived in the islands.

"I've used this knife almost every day since you bought it for me," Dad said. He was using the screwdriver to tighten the handle of the door on the rental car.

Mother and Rita sat in the back of the air-conditioned car. Dad drove and Sophia sat next to him. Outside the sun and the city were bright and hot.

"It's been a long time since all of us have been together like this," Mother said.

"Remember the old camper?" Rita asked. "Remember when it caught fire on that road in Georgia and we all had to bail out the side door. I grabbed the dog."

"Mom grabbed the food," Sophia said.

"It was just a little electrical fire," Dad said. "I can still see Sophia standing there with her fire extinguisher. It was almost as big as she was."

"I was scared," Sophia said. Dad was so big then and she was so small. She couldn't remember how old she had been, probably 11. She had been 11 until she was 14 because of discount fares. But when she was 14, her breasts grew and she became 18 so she could go to the discos in the islands.

With the money they weren't going to spend by not being able to go sailing, they bought a sailboard and racks for the car, so that they could take it back to the boat. They would be sailing after all. Sophia was becoming excited. She remembered her first attempt on a sailboard in the islands. She had sailed with the wind out beyond the reef and then couldn't get back. Dad had to swim out and tow her in.

When they got the sailboard back to the trimaran, the water was flat and slick as a mirror. Styrofoam cups and beer bottles floated motionless. There was not a hint of a breeze.

Sophia lay in her bunk with the hatch open and the fan on. She flipped through a magazine full of automobile ads. She would be going away to college in the fall and she wanted something sporty--something like a Porsche.

"My first car was the old Buick," Rita said. She was seated on her bunk, the lowered settee. She had a mirror propped in front of her and was brushing her hair. "They sold it for $300."

"To pay your phone bill," Sophia said.

"I was in love," Rita said. "You'll probably get a lot better car. You've always been the favorite."

"You're really screwed up," Sophia said.

"You know it's true," Rita insisted.

Mother's voice came from the forward cabin. It was loud. It was full of anger and frustration.

"Am I going to be 80 years old one day and still have to hear Rita complaining that Sophia is the favorite child?"

"I knew you would take her side," Rita yelled back. "You always do."

Dad stuck his head through the companionway.

"Rita, is your period about to start?" he said flatly.

"You always blame everything on that," Rita screamed. "I don't have PMS. Take me into shore. I don't want to be around any of you right now."

"No," Dad said.

Rita gritted her teeth and snarled. She stood up and adjusted her bathing suit. She crammed a skirt into her purse and pushed past her father through the companionway and up on deck. She didn't say anything. She let herself off the stern and with her purse held above her head she began swimming to shore.

Sophia came up on deck and stood next to her father.

"Go get her in the dinghy," she told him.

"No," he said.

"What if some power boat runs over her?" Sophia said. "Oh, I'll go."

Sophia started to untie the dinghy and stopped.

"Wow, is he hot!" she said.

There was a handsome young man in a blue dinghy rowing up to Rita bobbing along in the water. He was shirtless and muscular. He took her purse and she pulled herself up over the side. She was a good distance away but Sophia could see her stick her tongue out at her Dad before she sat down and looked away.

"Do you know him?" Sophia asked.

"He lives in the neighborhood," Dad said pointing to the other boats in the anchorage.

Mother was very upset. She came up on deck and saw Rita and the blue dinghy disappear toward the dock. She looked worried.

"She'll be alright," Sophia said. She put her arm around her mother and hugged her.

"Thank God she can take care of herself," Dad smiled. "Did you see her doing the sidestroke with that purse over her head?"

"It's not funny," Sophia said. "I'm worried about her."

"I'm more worried about him," Dad said. "You know how crazy she gets when . . ."

"You can't blame it all on her period," Sophia said.

"I lived with her for 20 years, 12 months a year," Dad said. "I notice things. I've lived with three women for 20 years and . . ."

"What are you doing? Research?" Mother asked.

"Who takes out the garbage?" Dad said, stating his case. "I see the evidence every month. You don't have to be a Ph.D. to put two and two together."

"You really think you're so damned smart," Mother said.

"Yes, I do," Father said, and paused to think. "And you're next."

Mother went below to her bunk and Sophia crawled in next to her. The hatch and the fan kept them comfortable. Sophia and her mother were about the same size, but Sophia's feet were bigger and they had different taste in music. Side by side, they lay in the bunk, twirling a lock of each other's hair.

While the sun was going down, they ate up on deck. They ate salad from the icebox. It ran off of the engine, and therefore it was also out of order. Perishables had to be eaten. They had a small gasoline generator, so they still would have lights, showers, fans and television.

"The wind is out of the west," Dad said. "it would have been a great night to go across. The moon is full and will be up soon."

A small motorboat with two men and a woman was coming out the channel toward them. The woman was waving. It was Rita.

"This is Willie and his father George," Rita said as she came aboard. "George doesn't speak any English."

"Muchas gracias," Dad said as they pulled away.

"I have to get dressed," Rita said. "A guy named Dave is taking me to a party on a boat called *Music Man*. He says he knows you. I met him on the dock."

"Was that the hunk who rowed you in?" Sophia asked.

"That was Renee," Rita said, as she took off her clothes. "Isn't he cute? But he has a girlfriend. Mom, do you have any tampons?"

"In the bathroom," Mother said.

"Dad, you were right," Rita said, and kissed him on the cheek. "Oh, you need a shave."

"Mom, Dad was right," Sophia said.

"You always take his side," Mother said. "The two of you like to gang up on me."

"I had this nightmare," Dad said. "I was trapped on this boat with three women and they all had their periods at the same time. Sophia, I hope you're late."

"Bite your tongue," Mother said.

"No way," Sophia said.

At night they lay up on the foredeck on cushions and in the nets between the hulls.

"See those stars," Rita said. "That's Scorpio. See the curve of the tail?"

She stood up and leaned on the forestay. Mother and Sophia lay next to each other on the cushions. Father stretched out in the net. The moon was up, and full, so it was easy to see the horizon across the bay.

"When I went to the bank," Sophia said, she was twirling her mother's hair, "they wouldn't cash my check, so I told them that I wanted to see the president."

"That sounds like something mom would do," Rita said. "I wrote a part in my play about mom. I rewrote the first act again."

"I want to read it when it's finished," Dad said.

"Did you know that Sophia wrote me a poem every day for two weeks while I was at school?" Rita asked. "Some of it was pretty good."

"It was all good," Sophia said. "But I think my best poem was the one I wrote in third grade."

"I guess that was when you peaked as a writer," Rita laughed. *"Summer is a wonderful time . . ."*

"A wonderful time," Mom joined in, *"for you and me. We could sail out to sea. Oh, what fun it would be. Just you and me on a summer day alone."*

"You all remembered," Sophia was surprised.

"When we lived in the house," Mom said. "I collected all of your poems."

"And mine too," Rita said.

"And your love letters too," Dad laughed.

"Dear John," Sophia teased.

"You didn't," Rita was shocked.

"Dear Tom," Dad added.

"Dear To Whom It May Concern," Mom laughed.

"I never wrote that," Rita smiled. "And who was Tom?"

"I loved that house," Sophia said. "I liked to sit in the living room early in the morning. I could hear the blue jays and cardinals singing in the backyard. I could hear the chimes from the Catholic Church in the center of town. When I heard eight gongs, I knew that it was time to leave for school. I'd always count the chimes. It was a wonderful house to live in and I felt blessed."

"I've missed you," Mom said softly. "I've missed both of you."

A small boat with a tall blonde boy pulled up alongside. Rita went with him to a well-lighted houseboat across the channel. There was no breeze now and the mosquitoes were out.

"I guess we'll sleep down below tonight," Dad said. "I'll start the generator. The fans will keep the bugs away."

"I'm being eaten alive," Sophia said, slapping her own face. "This sucks."

The generator started with a roar and stopped with a rattle and a cough. It didn't start again. Dad was cussing and cursing. Mom rubbed repellant on Sophia.

"No electricity," Sophia said. "No refrigeration. No showers, no fans, no wind. What next?"

"We have each other," Mother said.

"I wish that you had never sold the house," Sophia shouted. She rubbed insect repellant on her arms and legs. She wiped at her eyes and it stung and she began to cry. "I wish that you had never bought this damned boat."

"When you earn it," Dad yelled back, "you can decide how to spend it."

"It was our house too," Sophia said. Her father turned away from her and went to the stern of the boat where he peed over the side.

"He regrets it too," Mom said, putting her arm around Sophia. "He's so disappointed that this vacation broke down. He's put so much work into this boat."

They were all asleep on deck when Rita returned to the boat with someone named John. Sophia was awakened by Rita's tipsy whispered goodbye. Sophia helped her to the stern where they shared a glass of wine that Rita had with her. They were friends as well as sisters. There was a breeze now.

Sophia looked at her older sister in the moonlight. She was slim and beautiful. They leaned back against the cabin and their legs dangled over the side. Sophia's legs were longer than Rita's. It had taken so long.

Sophia remembered one summer in London in a park when she was half her sister's size. Rita had taken one of Sophia's small arms and legs in each hand and was spinning her. Sophia had stretched out her other arm and leg and was flying in a circle. It was thrilling, and she had never felt afraid in the hands of her big sister. Mother had taken their picture and it was packed away somewhere with the other things from the house. Sophia fell asleep thinking of London, and shepherd's pie, and Rita.

The next morning they were in the water as the sun came up. The stickiness and itching of the night vanished on the surface as they dove beneath the cool water. Each had a mask, snorkel and a pair of fins. Dad carried a pole spear.

Sophia loved to go diving with her family. She knew how the dolphins must feel. They dove down and examined the remains of an old fiberglass boat. The hull of the wreck was full of sand. A big gray triggerfish swam with them. A long silver barracuda watched from a distance. Dad swam toward it with his spear. The barracuda kept the space between them constant as Dad swam after him, but he never went away.

They dove again, and looked at the many beautiful small fish that lived in the old wreck. Under the ledge of the hull, antennae of lobsters waved. Dad went down slowly without his spear. He jammed his hand under the ledge and came out with a large lobster. They all cheered as he surfaced.

"Breakfast," Dad said holding the large spiny creature above the water. He twisted off the tail. There was a noise that sounded like screaming. The antennae still moved as the carapace drifted to the bottom, and many small fish came to feed on the pieces of flesh that still clung to the shell.

"Oh, no," Rita said. "I'll never eat lobster again."

Sophia swam down and picked up Dad's spear.

Many years ago, when they had vacationed on various Caribbean islands, she began diving with her father when mother was too tired, or disinterested in hunting for food. Sophia was still eleven and very small.

The waves had been very big and it was a long way to where the large fish were on the reef. The Frenchman who had told them about the spot said that it was 13 meters deep. Sophia figured it out in her head...more than 40 feet. That was pretty good for an 11-year-old. She was good at math like Dad.

Her father had dived down with his spear gun. Sophia floated above on the heaving surface and watched as he swan down and down and became very small in the large sea. He grabbed a coral shelf on the bottom and his head and spear gun disappeared inside a cave.

Sophia heard the metallic click of the spear gun and saw her father push out and swim for the surface. He was completely out of breath when he reached the top. He couldn't talk and only pointed down below. Sophia took a deep breath and dove down to retrieve the spear gun that her father had left behind.

She swam down, kicking with her fins. She equalized the pressure in her ears twice by pinching her nose through the mask and blowing out. She saw beautiful big fish that she had never seen before: iridescent blue, bright yellow, stripes of black and white, flashes of green, and red fading to gray, as she went deeper. A school of blue squid treaded water. The soft finger coral swayed with the surge of the sea on top of the coral shelf. There was the gun. There was the cave. She was out of breath.

Sophia turned and kicked off the bottom. She swam as hard as she could for the surface. She blew out until there was no more air in her lungs. The surface waived far above her. She kicked harder. Her father was floating above her. She swam to him. Sophia was crying when she broke the surface. The sea came in with her first breath, and she coughed it out. Dad was right next to her. She grabbed onto his shoulder and caught her breath. They bounced together on the waves. The next time Sophia dove down, she brought back the spear gun and the spear and a five-pound yellowtail snapper.

Two men came in the middle of the night, while Sophia slept below in order to avoid frequent thundershowers. There was a hot breeze from time to time. The men worked quietly and hardly spoke, laughing at metal clanking against metal, and grunting and groaning. In the morning the engine was working.

"Who wants to pull up the anchor?" Dad said.

"I'll do it," Sophia said. "Are we really going sailing?"

"It's just a shakedown cruise," Mother said. "Rita, help me run some safety lines. You never can tell what will happen once we get outside."

"That won't be necessary," Dad said. "We're only going out in the bay. And maybe, just out to look at the ocean. It depends on the wind."

Sophia was excited. They motored out of the anchorage without incident. Rita sat in her leopard-spotted bikini on the bow net and waved to every sailor she saw. Mother was at the wheel. Dad put up the big red and white Genoa sail. He pulled it tight with the winch and cleated the line. They picked up speed.

"Cut the engine," Dad yelled. "We're sailing."

When the engine stopped, all the sounds of the sea could be heard. The wind fluttered the sail and lines, and wires slapped against the mast. The water splashed by the hulls and a boiling wake ran behind them. Birds called from above.

Sophia sat next to her mother who manned the helm while Dad checked out various parts of the rigging.

"I'm so glad Dad's friends fixed the engine," Sophia said. "But why did they do it in the middle of the night?"

"They weren't Dad's friends," Mom said. "They brought Rita home from a party. One of them was a diesel mechanic."

Rita dozed in the forward net. Dad coiled some loose lines. Mom was steady at the wheel. She steered out toward the ocean.

"When we pass the lighthouse," Mom said, "I want everyone in the cockpit. Nobody goes out without a life jacket and safety harness."

"It depends on the size of the waves," Dad said.

The wind was from the side, off the starboard beam as they headed out of the channel. They were going much faster than they had with the engine, but the wide trimaran was constantly stable. Dad brought up two full cups of coffee from the galley. He had switched on the radio to the weather station: "seas two to four feet, winds southeast ten to fifteen knots, scattered thunderstorms."

Sophia walked around the spacious deck.

"One hand for the boat," Mother yelled.

Sophia grabbed on to the port shrouds, thick cables of stainless steel that kept the mast in place. She looked up and squinted against the sun. She counted seven cables and three lines, none of which she knew the proper name. She swung around on the shroud so that she was shaded by the sail.

Sophia went forward and sat in the other bow net across from Rita, who was now asleep in the sun. The net sank with Sophia's weight so that she was between the hulls. The water spilled by in a continuous torrent. A wave splashed as the bow dipped and threw up a shower of seawater that soaked her rear-end.

"I'm all wet," Sophia protested, and then laughed as Rita was splashed awake.

"That's our portable toilet," Dad said.

Sophia reclined on the net in the sunshine. She closed her eyes and felt the movement of the sea rising and falling, the boat splashing rapidly through the water. The wind whistled gently in time with the rush. It would be so easy to doze off, to dream within a dream.

BANG!

It sounded like a firecracker, a large explosive sound. It was so loud that both Sophia and Rita stuck their heads up from the nets at the same time.

"Keep down," Dad yelled.

The sail was full to the starboard side. Dad was standing on the cabin near the boom. He dropped to his knees, looking around frantically. Mother yelled from the wheel.

"The port shrouds," Mother yelled. "I'm heading up."

"Keep your heads down," Dad yelled, and moved across the deck.

The two steel cables and a steel plate that held the mast to the port side of the boat were swinging wildly and freely unattached.

"We'll lose the mast," Dad yelled, as he stood up to grab the swinging cables.

As the boat turned closer into the wind, the bow dipped on a wave. Sophia saw the metal plate strike her father in the head. It was a dull gong. As he fell forward, she could see the sky darkening behind them. There was a flash of lightning. Rita screamed.

In an instant, Sophia saw everything around her as she moved toward her fallen father. Rita was right next to her. The sail flapped wildly around them. The metal plate swung back again. Mother turned hard on the wheel and the sail filled against the wires to the side. The wind in the sail was holding up the mast. The boat rocked slightly to port, and the starboard shrouds bore the weight of the wind. The metal plate swung away from them.

A heavy safety line ran along the deck from the bow cleat to the stern cleat where mother and Rita had rigged it earlier. Father lay across the line. Rita checked the pulse in his neck.

"Everybody into the cockpit," Mother yelled. She tried to start the engine. Nothing happened. The sky had darkened and it was beginning to rain. It ran down their faces with their tears.

Father's wound was a large red welt that was darkening to an ugly lump on his forehead. The bow dipped and a wave washed across her father's face. His head rolled back and forth. His eyes were closed.

"We can't move him," Rita yelled. "He's too heavy."

"Tie him to the boat," Mother yelled.

The wind was picking up. It howled. The boat rose and fell. The sail strained and they were moving backwards. White caps formed all around them on the water.

"Sophia, come take the wheel," Mother yelled above the wind. "Rita, tie your father to the safety line. Here's a rope. Keep your heads down."

Sophia dodged the swinging metal plate and shrouds. She took a rope that Mother got from under the captain's chair, and passed it to Rita before she slid into the cockpit and moved behind the wheel.

"Keep us on this angle to the wind," Mother said. "I've got to tie off the mast." She looked behind them and could see the lighthouse. The wind was blowing the tops off the waves. Foam scattered across the deck.

Sophia watched the sail. It was still full against the spreaders. A large wave lifted the starboard bow. The bow dipped into another wave coming head on.

"Look out," Sophia yelled, and looked at the mast as the boat pitched into the trough.

Mother had gotten hold of the swinging cables and was hanging on them with all her weight. Sophia could see Rita's head slightly above the cabin top, but she could not see her father on the outer deck. Mother yelled something, but the wind was too loud to hear. The mast held.

Behind them the sky was black, cracked by lightning moving closer. The storm was now directly over the lighthouse. Mother still clung to the shrouds. Mother climbed onto the cabin top with her back pressed against the sail. She undid a snap shackle at the end of a line around a winch on the mast. Still clinging to the shrouds with one hand, she reached for the outer rail with the shackle. She snapped it to a block on the rail, and then struggled back to the mast. With the winch, she tightened the halyard until it was taut from the rail to the top of the mast. Then she tied the loose shrouds to the line with the belt from her shorts.

The mast was tied off and Sophia signed relief as the next wave broke.

"Heads up," Mother yelled.

Sophia turned the wheel in the direction her mother pointed. The sail flapped wildly. Mother pulled on a rope that wrapped the forward sail around a pole making the sail smaller. She then tied off the rope. Suddenly the sail filled to the port side and the boat turned toward the black sky. Mother winched the sail tight. The boat sailed into the storm.

The sky exploded as a bolt of lightning struck the lighthouse now in front of them. Sophia steered away. She was awed as the curtain of rain came across the lighthouse and it disappeared.

"Check your heading," Mother said, pointing to the compass in front of the wheel. She reached inside the cabin and turned on the running lights. The compass showed due west in its red light.

"How's Dad?" Sophia asked.

"We need to change course," Mother said. "We need to go east, out to sea where there's nothing to bump into."

"Is Dad alright?" Sophia asked.

"Rita is taking care of him," Mother said. "When I get up to the mast, head into the wind again and I'll guide the sail across the forestays."

Mother was gone from the cockpit out into the storm. The rain was heavy now, and the canopy leaked onto Sophia's shoulders. The plastic window of the dodger in front of her was streaked and spattered with rain. Sophia stuck her head out to see her mother, and the raindrops stung her face. She turned into the wind. The sail collapsed and Mother led it around the stays to the other side of the mast, where it filled with an explosion of wind. The mast held. They headed east.

The rain beat down the waves and the wind shifted, as the storm moved over them. Blackness became gray, and silver slivers of rain stabbed at her face, as Sophia looked out into the storm. The boat rode high on the heaving seas. Sophia tried to hold her course and keep the sail filled. Deep in the grayness of the storm, she could see the shattered whitecaps. There was no sky, only the endless gray. Sophia looked at the compass. The needle pointed northwest. In steering to the sea, she had followed the shifting wind and was now heading for shore.

Perhaps in the next unforeseen moment, they would go aground and be broken up on the rocks. Sophia turned the wheel hard to the right. The needle slowly came around toward the east. The boat was now sideways to the waves. The sail collapsed.

It came out of the blackness. A monster. A rogue wave so tall that Sophia only saw it when she looked up to see how the mast held. The small white line of the curl appeared at the top of a wave as high as the spreaders. The boat heeled slightly as the wave began to break over the boat. Water rushed into the cockpit and ran into the forward and aft cabins, which were still open.

The port pontoon of the trimaran was pushed down into the face of the wave.

"Hang on," Sophia yelled into the storm at her family somewhere on the port deck. She turned the wheel into the wave without response. The port pontoon suddenly rose back up from the water. The boat righted itself and they rafted sideways in the curl. Sophia's heart dropped with the sea as the wave passed beneath them. Her stomach rose to her throat. She screamed. She was soaking wet and tasted the salt of the sea on her lips.

"Are you all alright?" Sophia yelled into the storm on the port rail where she could see the white breakers racing away into the blackness.

Lightning struck the mast and the sky exploded. The thunder shook Sophia to the soles of her feet. Electricity ran down the backstay to a chain that hung into the water. A fire flared for an instant where the chain touched the hull, but it was quickly extinguished by the storm.

"Are you all alright?" Sophia yelled, but knew that the storm blew away her words. She tried to see the compass needle but the red light was gone.

"God, please help me," Sophia cried.

Another bolt of lightning crossed the sky. From its light, she could see the compass needle. They were headed due east. The sail was full. Nothing to bump into.

"Praise the Lord, amen," Sophia smiled through her tears. She steered at an angle to the waves. She took a deep breath and stretched her neck. From behind her she could see a thin line of light to the west. It was passing. The storm was passing.

Rita and Mother helped Dad into the cockpit. There was a huge lump on his head. They were all shivering.

"Are you okay?" Sophia said to her father.

"I ain't dead yet," Dad said.

The sky opened up like the curtain in a darkened theater, rising on a lighted stage. The sun burst through. They dried themselves with towels from down below, and put the canopy down. The sun was as warm as the sky was blue. Sophia stayed at the wheel.

"Don't let Dad go to sleep," Rita warmed Mom. "I learned that in paramedics."

Mother sat next to Dad. She wrapped a blanket around him. They held each other.

The wind was behind them now as they headed back to the anchorage. The Genoa was full. The boat rose up out of the water like a beautiful bird. It plunged down again as they surfed the big rolling swells from the ocean that turned to high waves as they came to the shallower waters of the bay. They made it safely back to their mooring.

"X-rays of Dad's head showed nothing," was the big joke for a couple of days. Mother retold the story of their shakedown cruise to everyone they met. Each time the waves got bigger, and the wind got stronger. Dad complained a lot about the engine. Rita kept asking him if he felt dizzy or felt like throwing up. The rest of the vacation was spent sail boarding, diving, and loving each other.

One afternoon they took Rita to the airport. It was a brief goodbye of tears and kisses. As they pulled away, they could hear Rita instructing the red cap in the care of her luggage. She stood in her long white skirt that Dad had bought her, and the red high heels that Mother gave her, and carried the leather bag that was a gift from Sophia. She was lovely, and shined amid the chaos of the departure gate.

Then it was Sophia's time to say goodbye to her parents. She had mailed in her final geometry exam to the correspondence school. She was now going away to college. Her father gave her a small package about the size of a lipstick but much heavier.

"Is this my gift?" Sophia asked.

"Yes," her father said. "I wanted to give you something that would last. Something you could use forever, for a lifetime."

Mother watched as Sophia ripped away the wrapping paper. She opened the small thin box. Inside was a red Swiss army knife, just like Dad's.

"I love you, Daddy," Sophia said.

"I love you too," Dad said.

Sometimes, Goat

It was dinnertime. They were three tourists in straw hats standing at the entrance of the waterfront restaurant looking at the menu written on a slate:

La Carte

Fish

Lobster

Chicken

Sometimes Goat

Inside were a dozen tables lit with kerosene lamps. It was hard to see what people were eating. The food smelled good. The kitchen was to their left. To the right was a staircase leading to a warehouse above them. The floor was dirt.

They selected a table between four men drinking the local bottled beer and a young couple holding hands.

The man, named Stephen Gary, ordered the fish. His wife, Veronique, ordered two lobsters. Their daughter, Marie, ordered the chicken. It was their custom to share.

"They're talking about drugs," Marie said, leaning back toward the four men. Her cheeks were pink from a day of sun. She was in her teens.

"They're talking about sex," the woman cocked her head to the couple behind her. She kept her hat on to conceal her baldness from the chemotherapy. She touched her husband under the table.

"Jesus Christ!" the man gasped looking at the staircase.

They turned and saw a rat the size of a dog coming down the steps. When it reached the bottom, it ran under the table of the young couple. The girl screamed, jumped up and ran into a wall. The rat ran across the floor into the kitchen. There was cursing and banging.

The four men laughed. The other patrons looked at the girl who was being comforted by her man.

The women sat with their feet tucked under them. Stephen Gary kept his feet on the floor and his hand on his knife, as he looked from the stairs to the kitchen. Veronique covered his hand with hers.

"*Mon hero*," she smiled.

The food was served hot with tropical spices, peas and rice on the side, and a helping of yams. It was delicious. They ate and joked about the rat.

"That's what I love about the islands," Veronique said. "The ambience."

"Typical tropical," Marie laughed.

Stephen Gary kept the knife nearby. They washed down the meal with rum punch. He paid the waiter cash, including a healthy tip. His wife approved.

They were standing outside with the warmth of the food in their bellies and the buzz of rum in their heads. The air smelled of the sea. It was all so wonderful.

"This is a meal I'll write home about," Marie said.

"Tell it true," Stephen Gary said. "Then it will last."

"Forever," Veronique added. She hugged her daughter.

"The Feast of the Rat," Stephen Gary declared.

"Sometimes, goat." Veronique said looking over her daughter's shoulder.

They couldn't stop laughing as they walked away from the entrance, leaving the slate with the menu behind them.

La Carte

Fish

Lobster

Chicken

Tonight Goat!

Starr

The old man first saw her when she arrived unexpectedly in the lobby of the small Paris hotel with Charlie's daughter Maxine, who had come up from Cannes for little Cousin Natalie's Confirmation. Natalie's father, Paul, had closed the hotel for all but family for the celebration. The two American couples with Maxine were uninvited guests.

From the far end of the ballroom, her presence had attracted the old man's attention. He was captivated by a most remarkably beautiful lady. He felt love at first sight. He felt his heart, his soul, and something else move.

The old man had now caught her eye, ignoring young Jacques, who was telling him about the American movie people. The old man directed him away. The boy went back to the front desk for more information. The old man and the woman looked at each other.

The other three Americans stood with their luggage, confronted by Paul, the eldest son who owned the modest hotel which he had renovated entirely for his daughter Natalie's Confirmation. As the eldest son, he headed the family by birth, and not by brains. He always needed to show his authority.

She walked across the lobby to the ballroom to where the old man sat, in a grand chair that represented his position of being the oldest member of all the families, and a veteran of the last war.

He knew that he was an old man, and that if he didn't always come to the point immediately, it was because years of experience, and the memories of three wives whom he had outlived, crowded every thought and idea. He was never alone.

She was truly beautiful.

"Pardon, monsieur," she said. Her accent was Parisian, but he was sure that she was American. She had an open smile and light manner. She asked him where to find the bathroom.

The smile on the old man's face grew broad, and his eyes grew moist as he looked into her dark brown eyes. Her face was tan with a touch of Italian olive oil. Her lips were red. Her hair was almost black and straight as an oriental. There was mixed blood in her.

The old man pointed to a sign across the lobby by the front desk, where Paul and Charlie were both talking at the same time, and Maxine was very angry. The uninvited and unwelcome guests politely chatted with the children who had come to inspect them. The old man asked the beautiful woman, in his best English, for her name.

"Starr," she answered, "like up in the sky."

She smiled at him and turned and walked across the room. She wore tight white pants with a white jacket. She had on good black leather boots that could be worn for riding. His second wife wore boots like that. She too walked gracefully. They would have been about the same age. In his memories, all of his wives were eternally young and beautiful. He enjoyed watching her walk across the lobby. If there was a God, then she was a blessing.

The old man was thinking about "love" when she came back a few minutes later. He must have spoken it aloud. He was not sure.

"Love?" she said, as if reading his mind.

"To be young and in love and in Paris in the spring," the old man said. "When I go to heaven, you will be the one I love in Paris in the springtime."

She kissed him on both cheeks. She laughed and returned to her companions who were being coldly escorted from the hotel by Paul.

"I've been kicked out of better places than this," Starr said. Her friends all laughed as they went out into the street.

The old man got up out of his grand chair and went to the window where the children were watching and talking about the Americans from the cinema, and the beautiful star, Starr.

"I touched her hair," young Jacques said. "It was like silk."

The old man could see her standing on the sidewalk. It was raining and she had her head back, feeling it on her face. The taller of the two men with her kissed her on the throat and hugged her. She let herself be hugged and continued to laugh in the rain. The old man put his hand over his heart. He had seen and felt such love before, three times, in Paris.

He sat back in his grand chair and remembered his second wife. She was so young, beautiful and dark like this girl. They also had stayed at a very good hotel, and every morning she would make love to him, and they would drink a small bottle of champagne before going out for breakfast. They walked the boulevards all day. At night, they danced and he would sip champagne from her slipper before going back to the very good hotel to make very good love again. In the middle of the night, he would awake to find her head on his stomach. Her long brown hair...brown, yes, brown. He laughed. That was his first wife with the long brown hair. And the third was blonde. Yes, almost blonde. He smiled.

Oh, how she had loved him in Paris. He married her because she made him feel as he had the first time: young and in love and in Paris in the spring. His first wife rode into his mind. His eyes closed and he dozed.

There was a commotion again at the front desk as the Americans reentered, wet and bemused. Maxine ran crying from the lobby out into the rain. Charlie was instructing young Jacques about the Americans' luggage. Paul stood behind the desk. He said nothing, his arms crossed, in front of the board that held the keys to the rooms. He would not move. Charlie went around him.

The old man was wide-awake and smiling when her eyes caught his again. He waived to her. She waved back and departed the group at the front desk to join him. When she was in front of him, she leaned forward and he kissed her twice on each cheek, and he put his hand on her hip.

"Thank you," she said. "At least someone here likes me."

"My first wife was an actress," the old man said. "She danced in Paris. I was a good dancer myself when I was young."

"I think there is still a dance or two left in you," she said, "but I'm no actress."

"You were in Cannes for the festival," he said. "You are so beautiful." He let her take his hand from her hip and she held it. She sat on the arm of his grand chair. He placed his free hand on her knee.

"My friends were there on movie business," she said. "I was there to bury my Uncle Frank, as he wished. He died recently."

"I would hope so," the old man said, "especially if you buried him."

His joke surprised her for an instant, and then they laughed together as he moved his hand down her leg and felt the smooth black leather of her boots. He caressed all his wives, who had all laughed so easily. He had always been attracted by humor in a woman.

His third wife laughed all the time. The youngest child had married and left the farm. There were those last years alone with her. He teased her and she laughed and no one heard but him. Her laughter was God's special gift to the old man. He knew that he would carry it with him to the grave. He would have it with him under the earth with which they would soon cover him. He would have it inside the coffin and would give it to the worms who would feed on him. They would replenish the soil, and the earth would share his special gift, for he would not need it then. The birds would eat the worms, and her laughter would fill the air. The world would be alive with her laughter, all across the sky long after he was dead.

He knew the pleasures of the flesh and the spirit. He knew that there had been difficulties, but he chose only to remember the joys. He knew so much now that he was old. He had tried to pass his knowledge on to his children. But they all knew that they were smarter than he was. So, he tried the grandchildren.

The old man thanked his three wives for what he had learned from them. The wife of his youth had taught him love of nature. They had worked the fields together. The second had taught him love of life. They had raised the children. The third had taught him understanding, which had enabled him to appreciate the gifts of the first two wives. They had grown old together. The women he had desired, he had married. No one had stirred him for a long time. It was so easy to play games in his mind with their memories, since his body was too old for games of love. He was now a spectator where once had been a performer, a hero, his own star.

Starr put her hand on his knee. He could feel the unique pleasure of getting an erection. He knew what it was. Now, he had to figure out what to do with it.

"Starr," someone called from across the room. They seemed to be leaving again. The children were bidding adieu.

The adults were preparing the table in the ballroom for a great feast. It was for some occasion, which the old man could not at all remember at the moment. He hoped that it was not a funeral. Maybe he was dead. Starr was an angel reaching into his coffin. But, was it possible to be dead and to have an erection? He hoped that it was possible.

Young Jacques, his grandson, had come to fetch Starr. She kissed the old man's hand quickly and went to her friends. It was so fast.

"Are they going again?" the old man asked the boy.

"I hope not," Jacques said. "Uncle Paul had us put their luggage in the two rooms on the top floor, all the way in the back."

The old man motioned the boy to move aside so that they could both see her. He could feel his heart in his chest pound, as they watched her round buttocks in the tight white pants move up the stairs. As she turned on the landing, he swore that she winked and blew him a kiss. Where had he put his glasses?

The young boy Jacques ran after Starr, and followed closely behind her as she ascended the stairs. The old man watched enviously, holding in his hand the warmth that remained from where her hand had touched his. He placed his hand in his lap, and held the warmth there. His three wives had touched him there; the third wife with her hand still warm from the kitchen. No, it was the second wife that liked to make love in the warm kitchen, while the children played outside in the snow. The first wife liked to make love in the snow. The third wife had given a secret love, which only the two of them knew. She was shy. The rest of the world would never know the magnificence of the love they had shared. He watched young Jacques run after Starr. The old man was warmed by his memories of youth.

Young Jacques wanted to remember this moment more than any other time in his entire young life. He wanted to remember her with all of his senses: the rush of the air through his lungs filled with her scent, the pounding of his heart in his ears in time to the beat of her boots on the wooden stairs, the fire that burned in his cheeks.

There was the aroma of lavender. She must have gotten her perfume in Grasse. The young boy smiled. He wondered if she could tell that he was not a virgin.

The old man had told him that there were times in life that made you feel happy to be alive. He should remember those times well with all of his senses. Life was made up of memories and expectations. Those wonderful times were to be remembered when expectations were so sorrowful that it was painful to think about them, and you could soothe yourself with memories until you felt happy to be alive again. The old man was very serious when he instructed his protégé to always remember "the good life."

Jacques watched Starr walk in front of him in an aroma of lavender, and he remembered Brigette. She had been with him under the apple tree, in the rain last summer. Her wet white skirt clung to her thighs and hips. The rain splattered against the leaves above them, and dripped on to them. It glistened as it fell on her face. Sunburned and tan, her neck was scented with lavender from Grasse. He was thirteen, and she was older. When he took off his shirt to hold over her head, she had pressed her cheek against his chest, so that he couldn't look into her eyes. Her face was warm and smooth, and her breath against his chest made him shiver. She then tilted her head back with her eyes closed. They kissed and his hand found the softness of her breast and his fingers caressed the firmness of its nipple.

The birds sang above them amid the shiny leaves, as she placed his shirt upon the ground beneath the tree. She rested her hips upon the shirt and pulled her skirt above her knees, offering him her legs. Jacques rubbed her calf, and then her thighs. He inhaled the scent of lavender. The old man had told him what to do if such an occasion should arise. He made love to Brigette as a man makes love.

As a boy, he followed Starr up the stairs. She was a real woman. He was flushed with desire. He memorized this moment in his brain, forever.

Dust danced in the light of the hallway. The smell of rain on the street came in from the open window. Jacques inhaled deeply, and watched Starr turn, as graceful as a ballerina. The memory. The moment. His souvenirs of love. She was above him on the stairs. His face was level with her hips and then her legs as she came all the way around until she looked down at him.

"What is your name?" she asked in French.

"Jacques," he replied. "I speak good English."

The sound of her voice echoed through him like a bell, and he was excited. He wished that she would say more to add to his memories. Her voice was warm, yet hushed, as if the words were meant only for him.

"Watch out, kid," one of the men said from above her on the stairs. "She'll break your heart."

"Do you want to talk with me?" Jacques said. His heart pounded. "We will practice our language. There is a small room near your room. It is quiet."

"I like his style," a man said.

She looked at him and smiled. In the shadows of the stairway, they both blushed. He could see a sparkle in her eyes. He knew they shared the same feelings.

"Jacques," she breathed his name. "I love you." Je t'aime. Je t'aime. Je t'aime."

"Fantastic," a man said. "You've still got it, baby. You could melt rocks."

They all laughed and then stopped to applaud her. Jacques was confused. Were they playing with him? Her words were sincere. He could tell. She came down next to him. In the same tone, with a rush of breath, she spoke to him.

"I used to dub movies in Paris, years ago. You know, put English to the French. Was I good?" she asked.

"Fantastic," Jacques said. "You were marvelous."

She kissed him on both cheeks and hugged him. He put his arms around her waist. He was as tall as she was.

"I want to ask you for a favor," she said, batting her eyelashes. Her eyes were dark and deep. Her lips were moist, her breath sweet.

"Be careful," a man said from the top of the stairs. "She's been married three times, and buried the last one."

They all laughed and Jacques joined them this time.

"Do you have a book on birds of France?" Starr asked.

"But, yes," Jacques said. Her smile was innocent. She did not pull away. She was an incredible woman.

The other Americans were on another floor. They looked at the numbers on the doors until they found those that matched the numbers on the keys. They paused.

"Are we still in France?" the other woman said out of breath.

"Starr," a man called. "Third door on the right at the end of the hall."

"Thank you, Willie," she answered him, and then turned back to young Jacques.

"Please," she said, "if you find the book, leave it in my room. I will read it tonight and return it in the morning. I saw so many beautiful birds on the trip up from Cannes. I want to know all of their names."

She likes the birds, Jacques thought. He remembered the birds above them in the tree, when he and Brigitte had made love. But he did not know their names. Now he wanted to learn the names of all the birds in France.

As he followed her down the hall, they came to the second door on the right where the other man and woman had gone. The man was waiting. He had a big smile, and was looking at the bulge in the front of young Jacques' pants.

"I think you've made a friend," the man said to Starr.

"Steve, behave yourself," she said, as she turned. "This is Jacques. He's getting me a book on birds."

"That's not all he's getting," Steve said. "Young man, please come in here a minute. I have the solution to our problem with the family."

He spoke in French and English, mixing the words in a strange accent. He took Jacques by the arm and pulled him aside. Starr continued to the third door on the right, which was open. Steve and Jacques watched her, as she turned back and smiled.

"Tell Willie I love him" Steve said, and added, "Because he always gets you." Then to Jacques, "You don't need a Mercedes if you have a big dick."

"Pardon?" Jacques said.

"There was an elephant and a mouse..." Steve began a story.

Starr laughed and shook her head. She blew a kiss to Jacques. He could feel it come on the air and warm his cheeks. He loved her more than his next breath. The door closed, and she was gone. There were no other sounds in the world but the beating of his heart and Steve talking.

As Starr entered the room, Willie waited by the door and closed it after her. The public world was left outside. He could resume their privacy, their secret life, away from the people she attracted.

The room was small with a bed, a dresser with a mirror, a chair and a night table. There was a window that looked out on the darkening day, colored gray by the rain. An overhead light cast the setting in a sepia tone that matched the chenille spread on the double bed.

Starr fell backwards onto the bed, making the metal springs sing. She lifted her legs and Willie moved between them. He pulled off her boots and rubbed her feet. She moaned with delight, and laughed, accompanied by the squeaking bed. She stopped.

"What's wrong?" Willie asked.

"They might hear us," Starr said. "I don't want Steve to know what we're doing. He'll tell everybody."

"He'll tell them anyway," Willie said. "So we might as well swing from the chandelier so he won't be made a liar."

There was a knock at the door. Willie went to answer it. There was Steve.

"Well, partner," Steve said. "This is another fine mess I've gotten us out of."

He walked past Willie to the bed. Starr turned over on her stomach, as he sat down next to her. Willie went to the dresser, where there was a small bottle of Armangac. It was open and he sipped from it and offered some to Steve, who refused.

"What did you do?" Willie said. "Have food flown in from Moujen?"

"He always knows how to get to me," Steve told Starr, who just nodded. "Moujen, the high point of our lives, a 14 course dinner for ten, and the money to pay for it."

"You used my credit card and signed my name." Willie said.

"We're partners," Steve said.

Starr began to laugh, and the bed began to shake.

"That's what I love about you two," Starr said. "We always have so much fun, and it's always something I've never done before. Our lives have never been boring with you, Steve."

"That's what I told the kid," Steve said.

"Is that what the mouse and the elephant are about?" Starr asked.

"You told him that?" Willie said. "Did he understand?"

"He understood the grand penis," Steve said.

"What?" Starr said. "You told him about a big penis?"

"There was a mouse and an elephant in the jungle," Steve started. Willie handed him the brandy. Starr listened to Steve tell the joke. "The elephant fell into a big hole and couldn't get out. Along comes this mouse in a Mercedes. He ties a rope to the back bumper and tosses the other end to the elephant. He puts the car in gear and pulls out the elephant. The elephant is very thankful and promises to repay the mouse some day. Well, what do you know. One day the mouse falls in a hole and can't get out. Along comes his friend the elephant. He stands over the hole, drops the end of his grand penis down to the mouse, who grabs it and holds on and the elephant puts his ass in gear and pulls him out. The moral of the story is, you don't need a Mercedes if you have a big dick!"

Starr started laughing and caused Steve to spill the brandy down his chin. Willie took the bottle from him.

"The last thing the kid said was that he only had a motorcycle," Steve said. "So, I guess he's no competition for me, partner."

"Oh, you're too much," Starr moaned, holding her stomach and laughing.

"No more. Not on an empty stomach," Starr said.

"So, Elephantman," Willie said, "are we going to get room service?"

"Go ahead, envy me," Steve said. "Well, I'm about to pull you out of another hole. You should forgive the expression."

"I'm hungry," Starr said.

"Let me explain the situation," Steve said and took another swig on the brandy while Willie held the bottle for him. "My partner! Thank you. The problem is that the hotel is officially closed for Cousin Natalie's Confirmation. Uncle Paul says we're uninvited and should be out in the street. Maxine's father Charlie says he won't hear of it or he'll take his side of the family and go home. So, we got rooms for the night."

"What about food?" Starr said. "Willie will pay for the rooms."

"I haven't had anything but Armangac and cheese all day," Willie said.

"I took care of everything," Steve said. "I'm your partner."

"You signed my name again," Willie said.

"No," Steve said.

"Whose name did you sign?" Starr asked.

"You two!" Steve shook his head. "I'm hurt."

Starr and Willie faked shame.

Steve pouted and turned his head away. They couldn't see his smile. He took the bottle from Willie without looking and sipped. He gave the bottle back to Willie and turned his attention to Starr's backside.

"Would you like to be spanked?" Steve said. "Spanked gently," he added.

"You can share the brandy," Starr said, "but some things are exclusive."

"So, limited partner," Willie said. "What, you should forgive the expression, is the bottom line?"

"About the food," Starr said. She turned and sat up. She looked at Willie and laughed.

"I'll bet he makes you laugh when you make love," Steve said. "Tell the truth. He makes you laugh."

"That's why I love him," Starr said.

"I can make you laugh too," Steve said.

"She laughs with me, not at me," Willie said.

"I don't have to sit here and be abused," Steve said. "I can go back to my room with the Mrs. and be abused."

"What is Mrs. Steve doing?" Starr asked.

"Mrs. Steve is in the bath," Mr. Steve said. "She's getting even for the bad service. She's using lots of hot water and she's already packed two towels."

"What a great idea," Starr said, and got up from the bed and opened the door to the bathroom. "But what about the food?"

"I took care of it," Steve said. "Do you remember that hundred dollar bill that I had in Cannes. The one nobody ever had change for?"

"Nobody ever had change," Starr said, and shook her head at Mr. Steve. "And Willie always left the tip."

"That's why he's my partner," Willie said. "He's great with other people's money."

"I was saving it for a special occasion," Steve said. "And this is it. I gave it to the kid to give to cousin Natalie. He'll be back in a few minutes and we'll be able to go down and eat at the party. Now, did I do good?"

"You done good," Starr said, and came over and kissed Steve on the forehead.

"Then, can I watch you get undressed?" Steve said.

"Out!" Starr said, and pointed to the door. "Back to your cage."

"Thanks for taking care of the kid," Willie said.

"That's what partners are for," Steve said. He got up from the bed and went out with a smile on his face.

"I just love him," Starr said to Willie after the door closed, "but not the same way I love you."

She came around to where he sat on the bed and hugged his face to her breasts. He set the bottle of brandy on the night table and pulled her down next to him. They embraced.

There was passion in the embrace. The passion molded them together in movement and breath. Their combined fire was greater than the sum of their two flames. For Willie, there was no greater place on earth than in Starr's arms. They made love with their mouths, hands, feet, skin, flesh and spirits. Their muscles entwined, engulfed and penetrated. The old bed creaked and moaned a rhapsody to their lovemaking. The tangle of bodies and clothes and bed sheets lay motionless when they were finished. Only their breaths moved. Only their hearts sounded. They lay satisfied. Willie said a silent prayer of thankfulness.

Willie went to the bathroom and drew hot water for a bath. The tub was large and white and deep. He looked forward to using it after Starr. He closed the door behind him to keep in the steam. He caught a glance of her lying on the bed smiling.

"I'm very happy," Starr said.

Willie sat on the bed and watched her take off the clothes that she had made love in. Her body was tan and firm. He loved the way she moved. She was a ballerina. Her dance was life.

"Without you," Willie said, "I would never have seen the poppies in bloom along the Mediterranean."

"You say the most wonderful things to me," Starr said.

"That's why you're with me," Willie said.

"And the fact that you have more than a Mercedes too," Starr laughed. "And why are you with me?"

"I guess, I'm right for the part," Willie said.

Starr kissed him on the lips, and then went into the steaming bathroom and closed the door. Willie could tell from her sounds that she enjoyed stepping into the hot tub. He sat for a moment, listening to her sigh.

The sun had gone down, and it was becoming chilly. He enjoyed the cool air surrounding his nakedness. He heard her just beyond the door, surrounded by the warmth of water. He loved life so much more because of Starr. She had made him aware of nature more than anyone else in the world. She found joy in everything, from the clouds and birds in the sky, to the fish and coral that decorated the depths of the sea.

Seeing Starr happy was Willie's greatest pleasure: greater than the scent of flowers, the movement of the ocean, or the consumptive climax of passion or victory. He knew that her laughter was good. Nothing in the universe could diminish the pleasure of her happiness. She elevated him to a place few men knew. If he believed in royalty, he would have been a king. If he believed in religion, he would have been a god. He only believed in his love for her, so he was content to only be a man.

Starr came out of the bathroom wrapped in a large towel, which they had taken from the big hotel in Cannes. Her hair was covered by a small white towel, worn as a turban. She was wet and shiny.

"Do you want to use my water?" she asked. "It's still hot." She quickly closed the bathroom door behind her, as small puffs of steam vanished around her. "I wasn't very dirty," she added.

"All right," Willie said, smiling broadly.

"What's so funny?" she said, inspecting herself for something hanging out.

"I was remembering you in Cannes," Willie said.

"When?" she said, looking puzzled, toweling off her bare chest. "Not when the paparazzi attacked me?"

She dropped the towel on the floor next to the bed and crawled beneath the covers.

"No," he said. "I meant Uncle Frank's funeral when you were topless, the puffs of white."

"Wasn't it wild!" she laughed. "Uncle Frank would have liked to have been there."

"He was there," Willie said, "And there. And there. And there."

Willie pointed to the ground, the air and then put a finger to his lips. They both laughed. With the finger to his lips, he tossed her a kiss, and went into the bathroom. He was immediately enveloped in a cloud of steam. He quickly sank beneath the warm waters of the tub. Her waters. He was surrounded by her.

Willie closed his eyes and remembered Starr standing atop a huge rock above the sea. Her white jacket was open down the front and he could see her tan breasts to the nipples.

A dozen long-stemmed roses lay at her feet. She wore her black boots and tight white pants. It was the same outfit that had attracted the members of the foreign press corps who waited for celebrities along La Croisette. They knew she must be someone. She was beautiful. It didn't matter who. Her picture was in all the papers the next day. The girl in the black boots. But, as she stood on the rock, with the roses at her feet and a shoebox in her hands, only Steve was there with a camera, and Willie directed the scene.

"First Uncle Frank and then the roses," Willie had said.

Starr took the top off the shoebox. Inside was a plastic bag full of ashes. Uncle Frank. She put down the box and then poured the contents of the plastic bag into the sea. The wind off the water caught part of the powder and blew it back in puffs of white that vanished into the air. The rest of the ashes drifted on the waves. Starr then picked up the roses and tossed them into the sea.

"Goodbye, Uncle Frank," she said. "We all love you."

The wind answered with a gust that blew her jacket wide open and she stood bare-chested to the world in Steve's photo, laughing as tears ran down her cheeks. Next to her mouth on one side was a trace of white powder, blown back by the wind. It was a kiss goodbye from Uncle Frank.

When Willie came out of the bathroom, Starr was still under the blankets. He crawled in next to her and she moved close to him. She was warm, and the back of her neck was wet.

"Do you think I'm crazy?" she said. "I just want to live a happy life. I don't want to hurt anyone. I want to be left alone. Is that crazy?"

"Not crazy," Willie said, "…eccentric."

"Thanks a lot," Starr frowned.

"But you can get away with it," Willie said. "Because you're beautiful. You don't have to make sense. You just have to show up."

"I know I'm not one of the ugly ones," Starr said.

"The paparazzi thought you were a star, 'like up in the sky'," Willie laughed.

"Don't tease me," Starr said.

"Do you want to be a movie star?" Willie asked.

"No," Starr said. "I really want to direct."

They both laughed. He kissed her. There was a knock at the door.

"Who is it?" Willie asked.

"Monsieur Jacques for Madame."

"That's the boy you were teasing earlier," Willie said.

"I wasn't teasing." Starr said. "I was flirting."

"Enter," Willie said.

Jacques was not surprised to see her in bed, for he had been thinking about such a thing for some time. He had not thought about the man. Jacques did not feel jealousy. It was more a sense of admiration as one runner to another, in a race when they both love to run and only one can win.

Jacques stepped into the room and closed the door behind him. He carried with him the book of birds that he had promised her. He was anxious to see the look of satisfaction in her eyes. It was a fine book bound in leather that had belonged to one of the old man's wives. The old man had been delighted when Jacques told him that she desired a book of birds. Jacques walked to her side of the bed and presented it to her.

"It is a gift," Jacques said, "from the old man and from me."

If he had been making love to her, he would not have hoped for a greater expression of joy. Her eyes were wide, her mouth was open as she sighed. She took the book from him, and their hands touched. The book fell open revealing the painted birds upon the pages, and she gasped at the beauty. She looked at him, and her eyes were moist and shining.

"Merci, merci, merci beaucoup," Starr said. "Thank you, oh so much."

Jacques watched her hands as she held the book. He imagined those hands holding his chest as she sat behind him on his motorcycle. He wanted to feel her arms around him with her breasts pressed against his back and the wind blowing wildly in their faces, as they rode around Paris.

"What about the food?" Willie asked. "I'm starving."

"But, of course," Jacques said as the man's eyes caught him staring at Starr's breasts, the covers having slipped from her shoulders as she looked at the book. Jacques could feel the blush searing his cheeks. The old man had once told him that a man was always hungry after making love. He looked directly at the man in bed with Starr, and they exchanged a smile.

"Since your friend paid the hundred dollars U.S.," Jacques said, "they have agreed that you may stay the night and I will bring you something to eat in your rooms."

"Thank you," Willie said.

"Thank you for not running me over," Starr said sarcastically. She sat up in the bed and wrapped the blanket around her. "What is this? Are we socially unacceptable to eat in the kitchen?"

Jacques did not understand her completely, but he saw fire in her eyes. She got out of bed completely nude. She went to the bathroom and disappeared behind a cloud of steam.

"Willie!" she yelled. "Hand me my green outfit and my white boots. We're going to a party."

"Her heart is Jewish," Willie told Jacques. "When she feels unwanted, she rebels. She is a formidable woman, and she always gets her way."

"I understand," Jacques said.

"Jacques," Starr called from the bathroom. "Please tell our friends to get dressed. We're going downstairs for dinner."

Jacques did not want to leave the room, but he knew that he must obey her. He retreated slowly toward the door, never taking his eyes from the bathroom, hoping to see her again, hoping to see her again nude, wanting another masterpiece to remember.

He knew that tonight was like a trip to the Louvre. It was a glimmer of creation. He felt a smile form on his face, as he thought that he was thinking like the old man, and he was only a boy with so much life ahead of him.

The man had gotten the clothes from the luggage and he too disappeared into the steam. Jacques went out and closed the door behind him. He felt sadness. He felt embarrassment at the family feud over such nice people. And then he was aware of anticipation, and the excitement began to build as he thought about Starr. What would she look like? What would she do? How would she act when confronted by Uncle Paul? Jacques was so happy to be alive. He would keep these memories all of his life. And when he became an old man, he would have much to tell the young boys.

Willie was standing in the hallway with Steve and Mrs. Steve when Starr came out of the room. She wore an abstract blouse of green and black patterns set in white, with a pair of tight pants. She was bare at the waist and snug at the hips. She wore the white leather boots that he had bought for her in Cannes. Her hair was still wet and shined, pulled back from her face. Her lips were red. His first reaction was to go to her and kiss her, but she had a sense of mission about her and was past him down the hall before he could move.

"Mine partner," Steve said. "Is she also so intense in bed?"

Willie looked at him and laughed. "If you only knew how good she was, you'd kill me out of jealousy."

Mr. Steve's jaw dropped as his imagination went wild. Then they both looked at Mrs. Steve, who was moving away down the hall. Steve put his arm around Willie's shoulder and kissed him on the cheek.

"We're equal partners," Steve said. "But somehow I think you're more equal than I am."

Willie, Steve and Mrs. Steve followed Starr down to the main lobby. Maxine was waiting for them at the bottom of the stairs. Young Jacques was standing by the front desk.

"We're leaving," Maxine said in tears. "Jacques, get their bags. I've never been so insulted."

From his seat in the main hall, the old man could see her again. In the bright lights of the lobby, her hair shown like a halo. He thought she looked to be an angel.

If she were the angel of death, he would love to go with her to eternity.

The invited guests kept walking in front of him, obscuring his view. They were mingling near the buffet table, but since the old man had not begun to eat, no one else had eaten. It was the custom of the family, age before beauty. To the old man, the custom was beauty before food. He had been waiting for Starr to return. He knew that she must come and thank him for the book of birds. It was only polite. He had waited patiently. With patience, one arrives at everything, or in this case, she comes to you.

A group moved in front of him with their wine glasses and brandies. There was a small band of musicians who began tuning up: relatives and friends who played the violin, concertina and guitar. The old man whistled to get their attention and motioned for them to move over to the corner where they would play. His view was clear again.

To the old man, it appeared that the Americans had been defeated as they stood comforting Maxine, who cried dramatically against the shoulder of one of the men. There was anger on the face of the other woman. The men were stoic and brave, but still full of sadness. He had seen the same look on the faces of Frenchmen and then the Germans long ago. But with every defeat, there is a victory. For each loser, there is a winner. And the battle is never over as long as one person resists. Viva la France. The old man watched Starr's eyes as she looked around the room. Their eyes met, and lightning flashed between them.

The old man winked at Starr, and she smiled. He felt the blood rush to his face, and his hand trembled slightly. His breath caught in his throat. He could feel his heart pounding, and his penis became erect again. Life was grand.

A path cleared for Starr as she walked across the lobby to the far end of the ballroom, where the old man sat in his grand chair. She walked with her chin up and her shoulders squared. The crowd grew quiet, as one by one their attention was attracted to the sight of this beautiful woman walking among them. She smiled and her eyes flashed with excitement. Electricity filled the air. She walked directly toward the old man. A draft pushed the fabric of her clothes smooth against her body. Her eyes never left his.

The carpet had been taken up for dancing, so that the tap of her heels on the hardwood floors was the only sound to be heard. Everyone was watching her. Jacques had worked his way through the crowd so that he stayed with her. She stopped.

Starr stopped in front of the old man. He recognized the scent of her perfume. He breathed in the lavender fragrance of all of his wives, in all of his memories. He knew that she had come for him. Her belly shown through dark tan in the space between her blouse and pants. The old man reached his hand toward her and touched her waist. She caught his hand and held it to the warmth of her body. The old man imagined that she too was subject to the same passion that moved him.

She was about to speak, but he said quickly, "Would you like to dance?"

She looked into his soul and said, "I would love to dance with you."

As the old man rose from the grand chair, he stumbled purposely for an instant and his cheek brushed against Starr's breast.

Willie was watching Starr from across the room as she went to the old man. Steve was standing next to him. He nudged Willie in the ribs.

"Did you see that move?" Steve said to Willie. "The man is smooth. But I'll put my money on Starr any day. That lady has the power."

"And she knows how to use it," Willie added. "Watch them. This is better than any movie we saw at Cannes."

"And it only cost a hundred dollars to get in," Steve said.

The old man stood erect, taking her right hand in his left hand, and placing his right hand on her hip. He was taller than she, and Starr smiled as she looked up into his eyes. He looked over to the musicians, who had quickly arranged themselves. With a nod of the old man's head, they began to play a waltz. The crowd began to talk and hum to the tune, but they stayed back and kept the floor clear for the old man and Starr. He moved her with experience and grace. She had complete faith in his lead and followed him effortlessly. They danced together, the old man moving closer until they moved as one, and his right hand was full on the cheek of her buttocks, when the song ended with a great flourish.

The crowd applauded. The men whistled and closed in for a dance. The women went to the tables full of food, where Mrs. Steve had already established herself at the head of the line.

Some children led Willie to a large chair in front of the fireplace. They had organized his service. A glass of wine was already waiting on the table next to the chair. Mr. Steve was being attended to by a group of young blushing girls who had surrounded him at the front desk. Maxine and Papa Charles were all smiles as they greeted everyone with hugs and kisses. Paul was nowhere in sight.

The old man clapped his hands and tapped his foot in a fast tempo. The musicians took their cue. He grabbed Starr by the waist and twirled her around the floor, forcing the crowd back into a wide circle.

They stepped and spun and laughed, as the beat grew faster and they grew breathless. Then the old man released Starr into the center of the circle, where she danced alone to accompaniment of the clapping crowd and the pulsating music. She kicked up her heels and swung her arms over her head. Her hands drew dramatic patterns in the air.

The women and children joined the circle, leaving their food at the table, so that they could keep time with their hands. They all watched Starr and were entertained by her dance. She ran around the edge of the floor. The men reached out for her, and she came teasingly close, but avoided each grasp until she got back to the old man. Then she took both of his hands in hers, and they spun into an embrace. The crowd applauded wildly. The old man maneuvered her back to his chair, where he sat down and Starr came to rest on his lap as the song ended.

The laughter was so loud that it brought Paul out of hiding. He pushed through the crowd to see for himself. There was Starr sitting on the old man's lap, kissing him on both cheeks. The old man had one hand on her bottom and the other moved up her bare midriff to her breast. She took both of his hand in hers and stood up. She looked around the room, her smile shining like a beacon as she caught her breath and looked for her next partner.

"I love to dance," Starr said in French.

All of the men moved forward. Paul was at the front. She held up her hand to stop him and shook a finger at him, with a mock frown pursing her lips. The crowd laughed, but some of the women let out sighs of disapproval, and went back to their food.

The old man chuckled at this brazen beauty who scolded the man who had tried to expel her, and then begged for a dance. If he were younger, he would carry her off to Paris in the spring, and they would make love all day and dance all night. He was thankful that he was blessed with an imagination that was still stronger than his legs. He closed his eyes so that he could see his three wives. They all smiled and were not the least bit jealous.

"Viva la difference," they sang in unison.

When the old man opened his eyes, Starr was dancing with Charlie. Others danced too. The music played on.

Willie watched everything from his seat by the fire. Young Jacques brought him a plate of paté with Dijon mustard. The boy pointed to a frame above the hearth that held a typewritten letter signed in a bold blue. The paper had yellowed with age, and there were two medals on colored ribbons beneath it. Willie recognized them as military decorations. Jacques reached up and took down the framed letter. The wall behind it held a white shadow, evidence that it had hung there undisturbed for a very long time.

The heading was "Supreme Allied Command" and the signature was "General Dwight D. Eisenhower" in his own hand. It was a letter of thanks, for saving the lives of two American fliers who had been shot down during the Nazi occupation.

"The old man is very brave," Jacques told Willie. "He walked into the hospital where the Americans were being held, and walked out with them dressed in women's clothes that he borrowed from one of his wives. He hid them in his potato barn for months before they could be smuggled across the border by the underground."

Willie looked across the room to where the old man was dancing with Starr again. He held her by the hips and she held his shoulders. They stepped sideways in a circle with the other dancers. Starr's head was thrown back as she laughed and the old man sang to her.

"The old man is the winner," young Jacques told Willie. "He is very brave, very wise, and he loves the women."

Jacques returned the frame to its place above the hearth. He looked at Willie and nodded his head in the affirmative, and Willie nodded in agreement. They both smiled and looked back to Starr, who was dragging Paul onto the dance floor. He was not putting up much of a fight, but it made a good show. The old man had returned to his grand chair, where the women served him wine and a plate of ham and potatoes. He was smiling and breathing heavily, waiting for his chance to dance again with Starr.

Starr danced all night. They all danced. The music set them in motion, and the food and wine fueled the engines. They roared around her, each man taking his turn with the beautiful American woman. Some of the wives disapproved among themselves and gave their husbands a sharp look, but when they came back to them after their turn, they danced together and laughed. Everyone had a good time.

When one of the good dancers like Charlie would dance with Starr, the other couples would move back and give them the floor. then another couple would replace them in the center as they kept time, and then more couples would move forward and the floor would be full again. It was as if waves of dancers ebbed and flowed through the night.

Starr spun in a swirl of flashing colors, her eyes a sparkling brown, her smile an arc of joy triumphant. When they sang songs in French, she joined them in French. Then she sang in English. Her voice was pure and loud when the band knew the tune but not the words. Steve joined her in his deep baritone. *"O – O – O – O – Oklahoma...."*

Young Jacques danced with Starr in the latest American style, and all the young girls watched excitedly, especially the tall blonde with the sad eyes whose name was Brigitte. She frowned until Steve took her out on the floor. Then she laughed loudly to all the world, as he sang in her ear.

It was very late when Willie saw Starr wave to him. She was still sought after by the men, but she resisted. Willie knew that this was his signal. He rescued Starr from the dance floor, and took her to the chair by the fire, where she drank an entire glass of wine before she sat down.

"Thank you so much, my love," she said, as she collapsed into the chair.

Starr placed her hand over her heart, as if to feel her own mortality. She closed her eyes. She was exhausted from pleasure, and knew that she would sleep well tonight.

Some of the crowd had vanished and others were departing with hugs and kisses.

The old man came over to where Starr sat. His mind was full of memories and his heart was full of joy. He lifted Starr's hand to his lips and kissed her fingers.

"This is heaven," the old man said.

"But I'm no angel," Starr said. She stood and kissed him on the lips. They embraced. The music had stopped. The party was over.

The morning light slipped into the room through white curtains. Starr slept next to Willie on the down mattress under the down blanket that covered them. All was quiet.

Willie carefully got out of bed and opened the window. The morning air was crisp and smelled of wood fires. He quickly retreated to the bed where he warmed himself against Starr, the turn of her hip, the arc of her back, the curve of her shoulder. Starr sighed. She breathed in the morning.

When her eyes opened, her face blossomed into a smile. First she pressed her back against him, and felt his hands move down her stomach to her thighs. She turned and kissed Willie's chest. She nipped his nipples, and he laughed.

"May I cut in," he said, and she laughed. "Is it my turn?"

"It's your turn," she said, and kissed him again, moving against him. He was stirred to a passion that rose in both of them. They began to make love.

The song began outside. It filled the courtyard and came through their open window like the call of a morning bird. The tone was rich and full. The phrasing spoke of knowledge and sentiment. It was Steve singing *As Time Goes By*...

"A kiss is just a kiss, a sigh is just a sigh . . ."

They kissed. They sighed. They made love to the song.

" . . . the world will always welcome lovers . . . "

Starr and Willie lay in each other's arms.

Steve and young Jacques sipped a bottle of champagne and talked about motorbikes and women.

The old man slept late and dreamt of Paris in the spring.

Other books by the author
at booksonnet.com:

Murder In Key West
a novel

Money Bay
screenplay

www.ingramcontent.com/pod-product-compliance
Lightning Source LLC
Chambersburg PA
CBHW020853090426
42736CB00008B/354